POLAND – A NEW POWER IN TRANSATLANTIC SECURITY

Of Related Interest

NATO Enters the 21st Century
edited by Ted Galen Carpenter

Explaining NATO Enlargement
by Robert W. Rauchhaus

Central European Security Concerns: Bridge, Buffer or Barrier?
edited by Jacob Kipp

Poland –
A New Power in
Transatlantic Security

Editors

MARCIN ZABOROWSKI

Centre for International Relations, Warsaw

DAVID H. DUNN

University of Birmingham, UK

FRANK CASS
LONDON • PORTLAND, OR

First published in 2003 in Great Britain by
FRANK CASS PUBLISHERS
Crown House, 47 Chase Side,
London, N14 5BP

and in the United States of America by
FRANK CASS PUBLISHERS
c/o ISBS
920 NE 58th Avenue, Suite 300
Portland, Oregon 97213-3786

Website: www.frankcass.com

British Library Cataloguing in Publication Data

Poland – a new power in transatlantic security
  1.North Atlantic Treaty Organization 2.Security,
  International 3.Poland – Foreign relations – 1989 – 4. Poland
  – Foreign relations – European Union Countries 5.Poland –
  Foreign relations – United States 6.European Union
  countries – Foreign relations – Poland 7.United States –
  Foreign relations – Poland 8.Poland – Military policy
  I.Zaborowski, Marcin II.Dunn, David H.
  327.4'38

ISBN 0-7146-5552-X (cloth)
ISBN 0-7146-8435-X (paper)

Library of Congress Cataloging in Publication Data

Poland: a new power in transatlantic security / editors, Marcin
Zaborowski, David H. Dunn.
   p. cm.
Includes bibliographical references and index.
   ISBN 0-7146-5552-X (cloth) -- ISBN 0-7146-8435-X (pbk.)
   1. Poland--Foreign relations--1989- 2. Poland--Military policy. 3.
National security--Poland. 4. National security--Europe. 5.
Europe--Defenses. I. Zaborowski, Marcin. II. Dunn, David H. III.
Title.
   DK4450.P634 2003
   327.43804'09'049--dc21

                                                2003007879

This group of studies first appeared in a Special Issue on
'Poland – A New Power in Transatlantic Security' of *Defence Studies* (ISSN 1470-2436)
2/2 (Summer 2002) published by Frank Cass.

Printed in Great Britain by Antony Rowe Ltd., Chippenham, Wilts.

Contents

Foreword

One of the original objectives of *Defence Studies* was to produce special themed editions from time to time. *Defence Studies* Volume 2, Number 2 (Summer 2002) on Poland and Polish security in the twenty-first century, edited by Marcin Zaborowski and David Dunn, is the first such offering.

It is our pleasure therefore to introduce the first guest editors of *Defence Studies* and their special themed edition:

Dr Marcin Zaborowski is a Lecturer in European Politics at Aston University, Birmingham, UK, as well as an Honorary Fellow at the Centre for International Relations in Warsaw and in the Institute for German Studies at the University of Birmingham. His publications revolve around the two broadly defined themes: The International Politics of Central and Eastern Europe and the Politics of Transition in Central and Eastern Europe. He was a holder of the NATO Academic fellowship on 'Transatlantic Relations and Polish Foreign and Security Policy'.

Dr David H. Dunn is a Senior Lecturer in the Department of Political Science and International Relations at the University of Birmingham, UK. His research interests include international security and American foreign policy. He is the author of *The Politics of Threat: Minuteman Vulnerability in American Security Policy* and *American Security in the 1990s*.

WYN BOWEN and DAVID HALL
Defence Studies Department
King's College London
Joint Services Command and Staff College

Preface: Dilemmas of a Newcomer

The end of the Cold War not only changed the nature of European Security, but also the meanings of what is meant by 'European' and what is meant by 'Security'. So much has changed in 13 years and so much has changed for Poland in particular that is transformation is symbolic of that transition. It was only 13 years ago that Solidarity defeated Communists in Poland in the first ever semi-competitive parliamentary elections in the Eastern bloc. However, in that short timespan Poland has evolved as an important new political actor on the European stage, a fact recognised by its admission to NATO in 1999 along with Hungary and the Czech Republic.

It is in this context that this issue seeks to evaluate Poland's new role in the security of the Euro-Atlantic area. Of the three new NATO members it is undoubtedly Poland's membership that has proved to be the most meaningful for the Alliance. With a population and size comparable with Spain and its location between the former Soviet Union and Germany, Poland represents one of Europe's 'strategic centres'. The history of the last century provided many examples of Poland's pivotal role in Europe. World War II started with Nazi Germany's invasion of Poland and events in Poland in the 1980s became one of the major contributing factors bringing about the end of Cold War.

With Poland's new position in transatlantic relations still a relatively new phenomenon, there remains a lack of informed opinion on the implications of this change. To many Western observers it remains unclear what role Poland is likely to play on the international stage. Is it likely to be a keen European, or a staunch Atlanticist? Or maybe, like Britain, it is trying to reconcile one with the other? Is the Polish Army fit to act as an ally of the West and to what degree does the legacy of having been 'on the other side' during the Cold War hinder Poland's capacities?

Finally, what do the Poles expect of NATO and what can they offer in return? This publication was born of the need to address the issues and dilemmas arising from Poland's new position in both NATO and in transatlantic relations. The issue focuses on analysing Poland's position as a newcomer in the transatlantic context and on perceptions in America and Europe of Poland's security policy and the role they would like to see Poland playing in transatlantic security. The outcome of these investigations is based on original research and as such it offers new insights into Polish security and defence policies as well as into the ever-evolving transatlantic security context.

Guest Editors
MARCIN ZABOROWSKI and DAVID H. DUNN

Acknowledgements

This work is an outcome of the project 'The Transatlantic Partnership and Poland's Interests' sponsored by the German Marshall Fund of the US – Grant # DC-003601 – run at the Centre for International Relations in Warsaw and directed by Olaf Osica. The authors of this issue would like to acknowledge the generous support of these two institutions and in particular of Craig Kennedy from the German Marshall Fund and Janusz Reiter and Janusz Onyszkiewicz from the Centre for International Relations.

Marcin Zaborowski would like to thank the NATO-EAPC Research Fellowship Programme, which co-sponsored his contribution to the issue.

The editors would like to thank Vanda Knowles for her assistance in preparing the final manuscript for publication.

Continental Drift?
Transatlantic Relations in the
Twenty-First Century

ADRIAN HYDE-PRICE

For over half a century, the close transatlantic relationship between Europe and the USA has provided an important factor of stability and predictability in global politics and international security. For most of this time, few mainstream political forces either side of the Atlantic seriously questioned the need for a robust transatlantic alliance. For America's European allies, US security guarantees provided security against a perceived Soviet threat without excessive defence expenditure and the militarisation of their societies, allowing them – in the words of President Truman – 'to get on with the real business of achieving a fuller and happier life for all our citizens'.[1] In return, the Europeans were prepared to submit voluntarily to the 'consensual hegemony' of the United States.

The US presence in Europe also provided a measure of reassurance against potential threats to the intra-European balance of power – most importantly, from Germany, its disruptive great power – thereby giving the US the role of Western Europe's 'pacifier'.[2] The NATO alliance thus addressed the three primary security concerns of the West Europeans – 'keeping the Russians out, the Americans in, and the Germans down', in the words of NATO's first Secretary-General Lord Ismay.[3]

Since the end of the Cold War, however, transatlantic relations have experienced some serious stresses and strains. The picture is not wholly negative. One positive development for the USA is that it now has a tranche of new allies in Central and Eastern Europe – the most important of which is Poland, given its size and geostrategic location, along with its Atlanticist foreign policy orientation. In addition, NATO's pre-eminence in Europe's security architecture has been strengthened both by enlargement and, more importantly, by its role in crisis management and coercive diplomacy in the Balkans.

Nonetheless, despite the density of political, institutional, economic and cultural bonds between Europe and America, there are growing indications of divergences between the two sides on a broad array of defence, trade and diplomatic issues. The 11 September 2001 terrorist attacks on New York City and Washington DC generated an enormous wave of sympathy for, and solidarity with, the American people, and for a brief moment transatlantic differences were put to one side. However, underlying problems remain and will not be easy to resolve. Policy-makers on both sides of the Atlantic have to confront a seemingly intractable raft of policy differences. One thing is certain: the transatlantic relationship will inevitably have to undergo a process of structural adaptation and political re-calibration if it is to continue to provide an element of international stability in the twenty-first century.

The article examines the overall health of the contemporary transatlantic relationship in the light of the differences that have emerged over recent years. It does so by outlining four scenarios for the future of transatlantic relations in the early twenty-first century. The analysis involves three steps.

First: an assessment of the nature and foundations of the transatlantic relationship.

Second: identifying the key factors driving its current and future development.

And third: outlining scenarios for the future.

The aim of this analysis is to draw out the implications of current policy options for the transatlantic relationship and to suggest ways of managing the increasingly complex agenda facing US and European decision-makers.

I. The Building Blocks of the Transatlantic Alliance

Despite regular talk of a 'crisis' in transatlantic relations, US-European relations have exhibited remarkable resilience over the past five decades. The reason for this is the overlapping and interlocking sets of interests upon which the transatlantic relationship has been based. As the then US Permanent Representative to the North Atlantic Council, Ambassador Alexander Vershbow, once noted, 'Democratic Europe and North America are bound together as no other two regions in the world. We are inextricably linked in a fortunate tangle of kinship, society, science, letters and commerce.'[4] This 'fortunate tangle' of shared interests has four distinct threads: security cooperation, political and institutional ties, economic interdependence and socio-cultural affinities.

1. Security Cooperation

At the core of the Cold War transatlantic alliance was the shared perception of a Soviet military and political threat.[5] Its importance for the overall health and vitality of US-European relations should not be underestimated. In the architecture of transatlantic relationship, security cooperation provided the steel girder in its central supporting pillar. The perceived Soviet threat provided the rationale for the establishment of NATO, and led to the stationing of substantial US conventional and nuclear forces in Europe.[6] This in turn had the added benefit of providing an element of stability in Western Europe by addressing residual concerns about potential great power security competition between Germany and its former strategic rivals.

2. Political and Institutional Ties

The transatlantic security alliance was buttressed by strong political affinities rooted in a shared anti-communism and in common liberal-democratic institutions and political practices. This political and normative affinity helped strengthen and enrich the main institutional link between the US and Western Europe – the North Atlantic Treaty Organisation (NATO), established by the Washington Treaty in 1949. NATO provided the principle institutional buckle between the US and Western Europe. With its elaborate collective decision-making procedures, involving hundreds of committees meeting regularly to discuss a wide range of issues, the Alliance functioned as a permanent and extensive consultative process between transatlantic partners. 'Beyond the definition of mutual defense of a traditional alliance', Henry Kissinger has argued, 'the nations of the North Atlantic have evolved a web of consultations and relationships to affirm and achieve a common political destiny.'[7]

This means that NATO came to serve not just as a military alliance, but as a form of political linkage across the Atlantic. As NATO Secretary-General Lord Robertson has noted, '[t]here was always more to NATO than collective defence. It remains an expression of something wider and deeper – a voluntary security community based on democracy, individual liberty, free economies and the rule of law.'[8]

US-European institutional links within the NATO alliance have been augmented by formal political relations between the US and the European Union (EU), and by America's participation in the Organization for Security and Cooperation in Europe (OSCE), but the alliance remains the primary mechanism for formalised transatlantic consultation.

In addition to these multilateral institutional structures, US-European relations have involved a series of close bilateral relations between

Washington and individual West European states – the US-UK 'special relationship' being only one example. The US has long cultivated this 'multiple bilateralism' with its European allies, even though at times such bilateral relations can undermine the multilateralism inherent in NATO.

One final political factor of significance has been the close personal ties that developed at elite level between individuals on both sides of the Atlantic. This was important in cementing close political and security cooperation in the face of competing pressures and interests.

3. Economic Interdependence

The transatlantic security alliance and political partnership was further reinforced by a dynamic economic and trade relationship. Economic ties between Europe and America grew steadily throughout the post-war period, and by the end of the twentieth century the combined annual trade and investment between Europe and America had reached almost $2 trillion. Today, half the goods and services produced in the world are made in the US or the EU. One in 12 US factory workers are employed in one of the 4,000 European-owned businesses in the US, while US firms in Europe employ three million Europeans.[9]

This deepening economic interdependence is symbolised by the merger between Chrysler and Daimler-Benz. As Stuart Eizenstat noted when he was Deputy Secretary of the Treasury, 'the relationship between the United States and Europe may be the most important, influential and prosperous bilateral relationship in modern times'.

4. Socio-Cultural Affinities

The resilience of the transatlantic relationship reflects the fact that it has drawn sustenance from a marked degree of cultural compatiblity and shared values.[10] Historically, the USA itself is very much the product of European culture and civilisation, whilst Europe in turn has been deeply permeated by post-war US culture – amounting to the 'Americanisation' of Europe, symbolised by Hollywood, McDonalds, Coca-Cola and rock 'n roll. These socio-cultural affinities mean that the transatlantic relationship has a depth and a popular resonance missing from the US-Japanese security alliance, or from the EU's 'strategic partnership' with Russia. They also reflect, and enhance, America's 'soft power' resources in its relations with its European partners.[11]

II. Strains in the Transatlantic Relationship

Despite the strong foundations and mutually supporting pillars of the transatlantic relationship, there is no hiding the fact that with the end of the Cold War, US-European relations have entered a new and troubled phase. Talk of 'continental drift' has become ever more widespread, as relations across the Atlantic have become increasingly more fractious. Whilst periodic 'crises' have been a perennial feature of transatlantic relations, a compelling case can be made for arguing that the current strains besetting US-European relations stem from fundamentally different – and less easily resolvable – causes than in the past. 'The early crises within the Alliance', Henry Kissinger has argued, 'were generally in the nature of family disputes, having to do with differing interpretations of the requirements of an agreed common security. Today the very definition of common security and, indeed, of common purpose is being questioned.'[12] The strains in transatlantic relations are evident in all its four pillars – security, political, economic and socio-cultural:

1. Security Relations

The fundamental problem for transatlantic relations following the end of the East–West conflict is that there is no 'clear and present danger' compelling the allies to put aside their differences in the face of a mutually shared external threat. Although there are many international and regional security problems facing both America and Europe (not least, international terrorism of the sort perpetrated by Osama bin Laden's al-Qa'ida network), there is little consensus on how best to respond to and manage these problems.

The security agenda is becoming more diffuse, multifaceted and complex, as clear 'threats' to national and alliance security give way to more ambiguous and imprecise 'risks and challenges' (such as poverty and corruption in the developing world, or global environmental degradation). This more diffuse and complex security agenda makes the task of developing a common transatlantic approach to global problems increasingly problematic. The problem here is that,

> For the United States, foreign policy is first and foremost about threats – both traditional threats (including possible military or political subversion of US friends and allies by countries that are hostile to US interests) and new threats resulting from the proliferation of weapons of mass destruction, the growing power of terrorist groups and other non-state actors, and the increasing vulnerability of US society to direct attack. For Europe, the foreign policy agenda is much broader, including dealing with actual threats to human security resulting from food diseases and intemperate

weather, addressing a new set of challenges arising in a globalized
world and building on new opportunities to consolidate democracy
in Europe and beyond.[13]

Underlying this is a fundamental asymmetry in transatlantic relations:
while the USA has global interests and concerns, the EU and most
European countries have regional interests. Although deepening
interdependence and the emergence of an increasingly globalised
economy make it imperative for European countries to look beyond their
immediate regional horizons, Europe's engagement with the outside
world is qualitatively and quantitatively different from that of the USA.

This asymmetry, coupled with significant transatlantic differences in
strategic culture and security thinking, has manifested itself in different
American and European approaches to a whole range of international
security problems. Two examples serve to illustrate broader divergence in
approaches to international security: first, the US penchant for identifying
'rogue states' (otherwise called 'states of concern') as the cause of complex
regional problems, and second, the US propensity to resort to military
coercion at an earlier stage of crisis management than many European
states would deem appropriate.[14]

These differences are reflected in divergent policies towards 'rogue
states' such as Iran, Iraq and North Korea – President Bush's 'axis of evil'.
Thus for example the US bombing of Baghdad in February 2001 was
condemned by French foreign minister Hubert Vedrine as having 'no
basis in international law'. 'At the root of these transatlantic differences',
Professor Stephan Bierling has suggested, 'are divergent perceptions of
what role to play on the world stage. The United States sees itself as a
global disciplinarian, willing to use its superior military capability as
necessary to ensure the primacy of its notion of stability and human rights.
The European Union's interests, on the other hand, are first and foremost
regional and, with its lesser military capability, the EU depends on the
forces of diplomacy and trade to serve them.'[15]

The problem lies with both sides. The US has all too often appeared
arrogant, insensitive and unilateralist, while the Europeans have elevated
their relative lack of hard power resources to a virtue, and criticised US
policy even though they have failed to develop realist policies to tackle
proliferation or conflict in the Middle East. If the US is often over-bearing
and arrogant, its European allies have often been irresponsible, smug and
complacent.

Differences over conflict management and international security were
most apparent in the early 1990s over the Bosnian war – a period which

witnessed the worst deterioration in transatlantic relations since the Suez war.[16] The crisis in the Balkans in the 1990s demonstrated the EU's failure to manage, let alone resolve, the violent break-up of Yugoslavia, and the benefits that robust US leadership can offer as a catalyst for action by the Europeans – who have shouldered the main military and economic burden of post-conflict rehabilitation in Bosnia since the signing of the Dayton peace accords.[17]

It is hard to disagree with Assistant US Secretary of State Richard Holbrooke's assessment that 'The lessons of Bosnia are clear for all to see. Unless the United States is willing to put its political and military muscle behind the quest for solutions to European instability, nothing really gets done.'[18]

At the same time, the experience of the Balkans suggests that there can be no military 'quick-fix' to complex regional conflicts, which require a long-term commitment of the international community to 'nation-building' and post-conflict rehabilitation – a lesson all too relevant to Afghanistan.

Over recent years, transatlantic divisions on security and defence issues have been most evident from three policy areas: Ballistic Missile Defense (BMD), the future of NATO and the EU's Common European Security and Defence Policy (ESDP).

European concerns over BMD have centred on the political consequences of a unilateral US rejection of the Anti-Ballistic Missile Treaty and fears about the 'decoupling' of US and European security.

As regards NATO, divisions have emerged over the future role of the organisation in global crisis management (an issue linked with differences over the need for an explicit UN Security Council mandate), enlargement and burden-sharing (a long-standing grievance). More fundamentally, there is no clear agreement on the underlying purpose and rationale of the Alliance in the post-Cold War world. Henry Kissinger has formulated the problem succinctly: although European leaders have reaffirmed their commitment to Atlantic ties, he notes, the question remains, 'whether the Alliance is still considered the expression of a common destiny or whether it is turning into a safety net for essentially national or regional policies. The leaders of both sides of the Atlantic face no more important challenges than to answer this question.'[19]

Finally, transatlantic differences over NATO are linked to those over the EU's aspiration to develop its own military crisis management capability autonomously from that of the USA. All these tensions touch on issues fundamental to European and global security, and reflect the fact that there is no longer a 'clear and present danger' around which the allies on both sides of the Atlantic can unite.

2. Political and Institutional Differences

The differences in security policy outlined above are compounded by a deepening transatlantic divide on political and institutional issues. The fundamental cause of the current malaise in transatlantic relations is the growing American preference for unilateralism in its foreign and security policy. This American unilateralism is the cancer at the heart of the alliance, and in the medium to long term, is incompatible with a viable US-European partnership.

The lack of consensus on fundamental issues of global governance stems from the different geopolitical contexts and historical experiences of the US and Europe.

European countries – by virtue of their size, history and political experience – are, by and large, firm supporters of multilateralism. Living in a densely populated geographical area characterised by a high degree of economic and societal interdependence, most European countries are accustomed to working together in multilateral structures to find mutually beneficial solutions to shared concerns. This has encouraged the emergence of a tightly woven web of multilateral institutions in Europe, from the OSCE and the EU, to sub-regional organisations such as the Visegrad group and the Council of Baltic Sea States.

The USA, on the other hand, occupies a large and spacious continent, and its two immediate neighbours are relatively powerless. At the same time, the US is powerful enough to get its way in many situations without the inconvenience of having to engage in multilateral negotiations with comparable powers. With the end of the Cold War, the US has become increasingly conscious of its relative power in its 'unipolar' moment, and is less and less willing to work with other states to strengthen global governance and tackle shared global problems. On the contrary, Washington shows increasing signs of frustration and disillusionment with multilateral institutions, which it perceives as being bureaucratic, ponderous and inefficient.

The tendency for the United States to assert its 'national interests' at the expense of global governance was apparent during the Clinton years, but is even more characteristic of the Bush administration. In pursuit of its short-term 'national interests', the USA has refused to ratify the Comprehensive Test Ban Treaty (CTBT), the Kyoto accords and the Chemical and Biological Weapons Convention. The US Senate refusal to ratify the CTBT on 13 October 1999 came after a joint appeal by Prime Minister Blair, Chancellor Schröder and President Chirac, and demonstrated the strength of unilateralist sentiment in Washington.[20] This decision undermined US credibility as an advocate of arms control and has weakened the prospects for future arms control agreements more generally. This is not in the interest of Europe – nor even, of the US itself. In the medium to long term, this form of assertive US unilateralism is incompatible with a healthy transatlantic partnership. It will also erode the moral and political capital upon which US leadership has been based throughout the post-war period.

European frustration with US unilateralism has been growing over recent years, and is one motivation for a more cohesive Common Foreign and Security Policy (CFSP). While most West European governments – with the notable exception of the French – were willing to kow-tow to the Americans during the Cold War because of the over-riding need for US security guarantees, this is less and less the case as the EU evolves into a more coherent political, economic and monetary actor.

As will be discussed later in this essay, the structural balance of power between the US and Europe has changed considerably since the early Cold War years, and old-style US 'leadership' will be less and less effective as Europeans gain more self-confidence and self-awareness. This has been recognised by some more clear-sighted officials in US administrations, past and present. For example, in his speech at Georgetown University on 19 October 2000, Clinton's National Security Advisor Samuel R. Berger formulated the problem in the following terms. 'What threatens to alienate our friends', he said, 'is not that we are wealthy and powerful, but that despite our wealth and power we do not meet our obligations to the UN, or devote more of our GDP (gross domestic product) to the reduction of global poverty, or ratify treaties we urge others to adopt.' 'There may be no real threat to our power today', he continued, 'But if we use power in a way that antagonises our friends and dishonours our commitments, we will lose our authority – and our power will mean very little.' His conclusion was that 'to remain strong, we must be a hyperpower our friends and allies can depend on'.[21]

3. Economic and Trade Issues

One unfortunate feature of transatlantic relations over the last decade has been the growth of trade disputes and economic rivalry. During the Cold War, similar conflicts were minimised given the need to preserve a united front in the face of a perceived external threat. Today, however, this external cement has gone. Moreover, Economic and Monetary Union (EMU) has made the EU more of an economic rival to the USA. It is against the background of this changed structural balance of economic power that a series of trade disputes have been fought out. Over recent years, the US has levied more than $300 million worth of sanctions on

European imports in disputes over trade in beef and bananas. The EU, meanwhile, has threatened to impose up to $4 billion of sanctions against the United States unless it abolishes a tax break for American exporters.

In addition, the EU Trade Commissioner, Leon Brittan, has strongly criticised the Helms-Burton Act (which provided for legal actions against foreign companies with investments in Cuba) as 'extra-territorial and expropriatory', and in breach of US international obligations. Brittan also accused the US of setting back the cause of global economic liberalisation and jeopardising the multilateral trade system by their unilateral imposition of trade sanctions against Iran and Libya.[22]

Another source of contention is the D'Amato/Kennedy Act which sought to penalise international companies investing in Iran or Libya's oil and gas industries. This presented a direct threat to major economic interests in Italy, France and Germany.[23]

US-EU differences over trade issues also led to the failure to restart negotiations in late 1999 during a rancorous meeting of the World Trade Organization (WTO) in Seattle (30 November–3 December 1999). The main sources of disagreement were biotechnology and agriculture, given US pressure on the EU to open its markets to Genetically Modified Organisms (GMOs), despite wide public concern in Europe about their long-term implications for the environment and health.

4. Socio-Cultural Divides

Alongside political, economic and security tensions, transatlantic relations have experienced an emerging socio-cultural divide. By the close of the twentieth century, it was clear that there are many profound differences between US and European society. The American model of liberal free market economies with minimal regulation sits uneasily with the Rhineland model of social market economics. Even the UK, which aped many of the de-regulation tendencies of America in the Thatcher years, has a very different model of welfare provision and labour market regulation than the US.

The different social, cultural and normative values in America and Europe are also high-lighted by differences over the death penalty and gun control. As Nicole Gnesotto, Director of the WEU Institute for Security Studies has noted, 'When it comes to those shared values that are considered to be the basis of the alliance of Western democracies, the divergences that abound in US and European policy – over the death penalty, the lack of gun control, social welfare, protection of the environment, development aid or multilateralism – signal radically different types of society.'[24]

The concern felt by many Europeans about this new form of continental drift is apparent from the remarks of Rafael Estrella, a Spanish legislator and president of the North Atlantic Treaty Organisation parliamentary assembly. 'There is a new generation coming up', he has pointed out, 'that has no memory of the Soviet threat as a basis of a special relationship with the United States. Young people think of America in terms of the culprit behind the death penalty, global warming, the bombs over Baghdad and the use of depleted uranium weapons in Kosovo. For governing coalitions in Europe, it means when the next international crisis comes, it will be much harder to rally people behind the United States.'[25]

The social, cultural and normative differences generated by the different life experiences of Americans and Europeans are very worrying. As one commentator has written, 'experience shows that conflicts that involve a nation's cultural identity have far more destructive power in bilateral relations than disputes over objective interests for which compromises can be found'.[26]

The Bush Administration

Worries over the current state of transatlantic relations have been exacerbated by the change of administration in Washington in early 2001.[27] It has often been noted that the honeymoon period for a new US administration is always a nightmare for Europe, and this is certainly the case with the new Bush administration. Stresses and strains in US-European relations during the Clinton administration were in part ameliorated given President Clinton's skilful personal diplomacy and his administration's willing to try and find some means of accommodating the concerns of its European allies. Nonetheless, Clinton's foreign policy abilities only developed after a painful teething period, and could not prevent divisions from emerging with the Europeans on a whole raft of issues.

The inauguration of the 43rd President of the United States, George W. Bush, in January 2001, may herald the start of a healing of transatlantic divisions and the birth of a new atlantic partnership, but it seems more likely to widen existing breaches. The Bush administration has generated considerable consternation in European capitals given its articulation of a foreign and security policy based on a robust pursuit of America's 'national interests'. This 'America First' policy has already led the US to withdraw from the Kyoto accords and to refuse to ratify the Chemical and Biological Weapons Convention, and to press ahead with Ballistic Missile Defense regardless of the concerns of other countries, including America's NATO allies.

On coming to power, Bush said that he wished to give top priority to relations with America's immediate neighbours, Mexico and Canada.

These were the first foreign leaders that Bush met after coming to office (February 2001). Bush has emphasised the importance he attaches to Latin America and to the continued strict isolation of Cuba, and to the fast track mandate for expanding the North American Free Trade Association (NAFTA).

This focus on America's 'near abroad' has worries many European policy-makers who are concerned the Bush's foreign policy team underestimate the problems plaguing transatlantic relations. They have argued that he should turn his attention to fixing a commercial, political and security partnership they believe Americans have taken for granted for too long.[28] Whether the Bush administration, after a painful learning period, will take this on board and devote the necessary time and energy to injecting new life into the transatlantic relationship remains to be seen. Given their preference for pushing America's national interests at virtually any diplomatic and political cost, the prospects for resolving some of the tensions in US-European relations appear bleak.

European concerns about the Bush team centre on growing perceptions of US unilateralism, even arrogance. This is reflected in the Bush team's hostility to the Comprehensive Test Ban Treaty (CTBT), the International Criminal Court and the global warming treaty. This hostility has deepened European convictions that the US now places itself above the constraints of international law and multilateral institutions – first and foremost the UN. As one senior German official has argued, '[a] lot of people on Bush's national security team come from the Cold War era and think the Europeans have to fall in line with everything they say. But the days when the Americans could manage the alliance as they see fit are over. They need to show a better grasp of how to compromise.'[29]

Transatlantic Relations and the Changing Structure of the International System

In order to understand the significance and implication of the current travails of the transatlantic relationship, it is important to grasp the underlying changes in the structure of power in the international system. The key point to note is that the balance of power relationships which existed during the Cold War in transatlantic relations has significantly altered, and this requires that a significant re-calibration of US-European relations takes place.

The end of the Cold War and the disintegration of the Soviet Union left the USA as the preponderant political, economic and military power in the international system. Some have spoken of America enjoying a unique 'unipolar' moment. Whatever the utility of this notion, there is no doubt that the US bestrides the global system like a colossus, dominating business, commerce and communications. It has the world's largest economy, and militarily stands head and shoulders above any potential rival or coalition of rivals. By 1996, after cutting its defence budget back from the 8 per cent of GDP it spent during the Cold War to around 3 per cent, US defence expenditure was still greater than the world's next ten military powers combined.[30]

The problem, however, is that the US is not sure how best to use this enormous power.[31] Since the end of the Cold War a far-reaching foreign and security policy debate has been underway in Washington.[32]

At one end, there are those advocating close engagement with America's allies in order to tackle sources of regional conflicts and to strengthen international peace, prosperity and cooperation.

On the other hand, there is a growing mood of unilateralism among many. More seriously perhaps, Henry Kissinger has noted that 'America's pre-eminence is often treated with indifference by its own people. Judging from media coverage and congressional sentiments – two important barometers – Americans' interest in foreign policy is at an all-time low. …The last presidential election was the third in a row in which foreign policy was not seriously discussed by the candidates.' Kissinger warns that, at the apogee of its power, the US finds itself in an ironic position. 'In the face of perhaps the most profound and widespread upheavals the world has ever seen, it has failed to develop concepts relevant to the emerging realities.'[33]

In Europe, the end of the Cold War and German unification has given a new impetus to the process of European integration. Since the Maastricht Treaty on European Union, three key processes have been unfolding: political union, involving the development of a Common Foreign and Security Policy, including defence; economic and monetary union, symbolised by the launch of the Euro; and enlargement, beginning in 1995 with three European Free Trade Association states, and now planned to embrace a dozen countries, primarily drawn from Central and Eastern Europe. The cumulative effect of these developments has been to shift the relative balance of political and economic power between the USA and 'Europe'[34] – not least, because the EU is now larger than the USA in both population and GDP. 'Europe' still might not speak with one voice, but it does exert a much greater and more coherent 'presence' in the international system than it did in previous decades.

Above all, Europe no longer needs the US security guarantee. The continent is, for the most part, at peace, and Russia no longer presents a credible security threat. The EU is dynamic, growing in self-confidence and enlarging. This cannot but lead to change in the character of the transatlantic relationship and to a more fundamental re-calibration of US-European relations.

III. Scenarios for the Future of Transatlantic Relations

In this final section we shall consider four scenarios for the future of transatlantic relations. These are designed to provide a template for thinking about the implications of policy choices for the health and viable of US-European relations in the early twenty-first century.

1. Reborn Partnership

This is the most optimistic – but not necessarily most likely – scenario. Such an outcome would in many respects meet the fundamental interests of both sides. The USA and its European allies have benefited enormously from the strength and vitality of the transatlantic relationship over the last half a century and more. It remains an important pillar of global security and cooperation. Both sides share many common interests and concerns, in the political, economic, cultural and security spheres. Despite sources of tension and strains in the relationship, therefore, it remains important for both sides. Only on the basis of cooperation and partnership can common security concerns be managed and addressed in a pro-active manner: namely, 'rogue' states, proliferation, terrorism, regional conflicts in the Middle East and the Balkans.

To realise this scenario, US and European elites would have to cultivate a genuine transatlantic **partnership**. This would require a greater degree of coherence and political cooperation among European states within the framework of the EU, and an American willingness to forego demands for unilateral 'leadership' rather than multilateral partnership.

There are influential voices on both sides of the Atlantic arguing precisely for such a re-forged partnership as the basis for a healthy and mutually beneficial transatlantic relationship.[35] At an address to the US Military Academy at West Point on 14 September 1999, for example, Assistant Secretary of State for European Affairs Marc Grossman called for a new 'partnership alliance' between the US and Europe, based on five distinguishing features.

First, it would be a relationship with Europe as a whole, not just the Western half.

Second, it would be a relationship in which defence and security are vital, but economic security and managing global threats command more attention.

Third, it would be a relationship that takes, as a mission, conflict prevention, crisis management, and heading off problems before they start.

Fourth, it would be relationship where the US and Europe share risks and burdens, but also the responsibility to find common solutions to threats and crises beyond Europe.

Finally, it would be a relationship that builds on the facts of globalisation and which was based on the perception that US and European economies and societies were integrating faster and on more levels than ever before.[36]

The problem with this scenario is that it would require demanding changes in the assumptions and foreign policy behaviour of the USA and Europe. For such a 'multilateral partnership' to emerge, Europeans would have to look beyond their immediate neighbourhood and engage with the complexities and demands of the wider international system. At the same time, the US foreign policy elite would need to learn how to listen to its allies and to respond in a constructive way to their concerns and worries.

Partnership is certainly incompatible with the unilateralism that has characterised much US engagement with the outside world over recent years. Cooperation and partnership will only survive and prosper if nurtured and sustained by a constant process of negotiation, communication and mutual help. This involves a willingness to make compromises and to reach consensus, even at the cost of one's own narrow national interests. The United States would have to distinguish between power and authority, and recognise that by asserting US power in a unilateral way, it risks undermining its authority among its allies and friends.[37]

Partnership would thus demand a policy of **'enlightened self-interest'** – similar in vision and generosity to that of the Berlin Airlift or Marshall Aid. Whether the current Bush administration is able to recognise this is an open question at present – particularly in the light of US policy on Kyoto, missile defense, chemical and biological weapons, CTBT and ESDP.

2. Divorce

The second scenario would be the most dramatic and unsettling. It assumes a fundamental change of heart in Washington and in the leading capitals of Europe regarding the utility of trying to patch up a shaky relationship and a decision to pursue more independent foreign and security policies. Such a development could be precipitated by a major crisis within NATO, comparable to that which affected transatlantic relations in the early 1990s over Bosnia. One precondition for a 'divorce' would be the emergence of a more coherent and robust EU, with the ability to conduct its own autonomous foreign, security and defence policy. This scenario also assumes either the dominance of isolationist voices in Washington, and/or a US decision to focus on its interests in its 'near abroad' and in the Asia-Pacific region.

At present, this doomsday scenario is unlikely. As one commentator has noted, 'The worst bilateral relationship between the United States and a European country (France) is still much better, deeper and more significant than the best bilateral relationship the United States has with any country in Asia (Japan).'[38]

There is no indication that the necessary change in foreign policy assumptions in America or Europe is on the cards, and its ramifications would be too destabilising for the current generation of foreign policy elites on both sides of the Atlantic to consider. There is also no prospect of the EU developing the necessary political cohesion for Europeans to contemplate divorce, nor any indications of significant erosion of Atlanticist sentiments in key European capitals (such as London, Berlin or Warsaw).

Nonetheless, it cannot be discounted if the current trend towards 'continental drift' continues unimpeded and if a major crisis in transatlantic relations were to develop – for example, a unilateral decision by the USA to wage war on the 'axis of evil' in the face of European reservations.

3. Continuing Continental Drift

This scenario would be the equivalent of continuing with a successful but unhappy marriage. The transatlantic relationship would continue to be important symbolically and politically, and would incorporate substantive formal cooperation and consultation on a range of foreign policy issues. However, the underlying sources of tension would remain unresolved, and both sides would have a tendency to 'do their own thing' in policy areas such as global warming, trade, Middle Eastern policy and relations with Russia. European countries would focus on regional concerns, and the US would pursue a more unilateral approach to foreign policy and limit its active engagement in multilateral organisations such as the UN or the OSCE.

This unilateralism would be tempered to some extent by an increasing reliance on 'multiple bilateralism', with the US making use of its 'special relations' with key European allies. NATO would remain an important forum for security consultation, and the US would continue to station forces in Europe – although primarily with a view towards wider power projection in regions such as the Middle East, Gulf or Central Asia.

NATO's own role in military crisis-management would involve limited 'coalitions of the willing', often without US participation, and many peace-support operations in Europe would be conducted in the framework of EU-led operations using NATO military assets.

Both sides could conceivably live with such an unhappy marriage for some time, but it would pose the risk of the relationship further deteriorating - threatening a slide into a messy divorce. It would have the adverse consequence that many global security problems – such as nuclear proliferation, instability in the Middle East or humanitarian disasters in the less developed world – would be dealt with on an ad hoc basis, rather than pro-actively and collaboratively.

This scenario could result from a continuation and intensification of current tensions in the transatlantic relationship, and unless significant steps are taken to address these tensions, there are worrying indications that 'continental drift' may become irreversible. One source of concern is that many in Europe are wrapped up in debates and plans for the future of Europe, and tend to place transatlantic relations on the back-burner. This tendency is likely to continue for the rest of this decade, given the challenges presented by EMU, EU eastern enlargement and the building of a European defence and security capability.

Another worry is that, as *The Economist* magazine noted, 'America's allies sometimes imagine that America's superpower status has transformed it, or ought to have transformed it, into some giant disinterested force for peace and good. But America is a nation like any other; its own interests almost always come first.'[39]

The problem for both sides is that if national interests are defined in zero-sum terms, or without considering the implications for cooperation with partners and allies, then growing divergence becomes inevitable. Viewed in this light, the 'decidedly traditionalist view of international politics – a zero-sum struggle for power between the United States and those that could threaten its territory, allies, friends or interests'[40] which characterises the Bush administration must be a source of concern among its allies in Europe.

4. Partial Rapprochement

A more optimistic scenario, and one that is less demanding than 'reborn partnership', is of a gradual convergence on a range of policy areas, without necessarily reaching a consensus on all existing disagreements. This would involve a concerted attempt to negotiate on a range of issues from global warming to arms control policies, and a willingness to accommodate the interests of alliance partners. The mood of solidarity and support that swept Europe after 11 September 2001 suggests that the political and emotional capital can be mobilised if there is sufficient political will and effective leadership on both sides. However, divergences over how to rebuild Afghanistan and over the unilateral US abrogation of the Anti-Ballistic Missile Treaty also indicate that this political and emotional capital is not sufficient in the absence of a willingness to reach consensus and compromise on substantive differences. As Henry Kissinger notes,

> A relationship of genuine cooperation implies that the two sides of the Atlantic are willing to modify their immediate short-term interests for the long-term necessities of a broader vision. But as Western democracies are ever more driven internally by short-term considerations, the constituencies for the long term shrink; the political rewards are for actions either which demonstrate immediate benefits or reward short-term passions. It therefore comes down to a question of leadership on both sides of the Atlantic.[41]

Conclusion

In Ibsen's play *Hedda Gabler* (1890), one character (Tesman) exclaims, 'But, good heavens, we know nothing of the future', to which Lovberg replies, 'No, but there is a thing or two to be said about it all the same.' Clearly, we do not know what the future of the transatlantic relationship will be, and what its implications for a country like Poland will be.

However, it is clear that US-European relations stand on the cusp of far-reaching change. Current stresses and strains reflect not merely disputes over specific policy issues, but a more deep-seated structural adjustment in the relative economic and political weight of Europe and America. There are worrying signs that continental drift will continue, but there are – as yet – no reasons to believe that a divorce is on the cards.

At the same time, given current political realities in Washington and Europe, a re-born partnership is unlikely because it is too demanding. The best that can be hoped for is a partial rapprochement. Yet even this will require that much more serious attention is accorded to the health of the transatlantic relationship than has been apparent in the years either side of the second millennium.

NOTES

1. Harry Truman, 4 April 1949 quoted in Don Cook, *Forging the Alliance: NATO, 1945 to 1950* (London: Secker 1989) p.222.
2. Josef Joffe, 'Europe's American Pacifier', *Foreign Policy* 54 (Spring 1984).
3. For further details see Adrian Hyde-Price, *European Security Beyond the Cold War: Four Scenarios for the Year 2010* (London: Sage 1991) p.120.
4. Alexander Vershbow, 'Preserving the Transatlantic Link', Official Text, Office of Public Affairs, 26 Jan. 2000, p.2.
5. For an analysis of the strategic significance of the transatlantic alliance, see Carl Jacobsen, (ed.) *Strategic Power USA/USSR* (London: Macmillan 1990).
6. On this issue, see Daniel J. Nelson, *Defenders or Intruders? The Dilemmas of US Forces in Germany* (Boulder, CO: Westview 1987).
7. Henry Kissinger, *Does America Need a Foreign Policy? Toward a Diplomacy for the 21st Century* (NY: Simon & Schuster 2001) pp.32–3.
8. Quoted in 'Europe Says US should Mend Fraying Alliance', *International Herald Tribune*, 24/25 Feb. 2001, p.1.
9. E. Antony Wayne, 'The EU: US Perspectives', Official Text, Office of Public Affairs, 10 Nov. 1999, p.6.
10. Margarita Mathiopoulos, *History and Progress. In Search of the European and American Mind* (NY: Praeger 1989).
11. See Joseph Nye, *The Paradox of American Power: Why the World's Only Superpower Can't Go It Alone* (Oxford: OUP 2002) pp.9–12.
12. See Kissinger (note 7) p.33.
13. Ivo Daalder, 'Are the United States and Europe heading for Divorce?', *International Affairs* 77/3 (July 2001) pp.553–68 (p.559).
14. For an insightful discussion on the historical roots of US and European attitudes to war and the use of military force see General Wesley K. Clark, *Waging Modern War* (Oxford: Public Affairs 2001) pp.xxvii–xxx.
15. Stephan Bierling, 'Clash of Cultures Loosening Ties Tightened by Cold War', *Frankfurt Allgemeine Zeitung*, 24 Feb. 2001 (English Edition, 47) p.3.
16. Brendan Simms, *Unfinest Hour: Britain and the Destruction of Bosnia* (London: Allen Lane 2001) esp. pp.49–89.
17. Simon Serfaty, 'America and Europe: Beyond Bosnia', *The Washington Quarterly* 19/3 (Summer 1996) pp.31–44.
18. Quoted in 'EU Reels at Charges of Disarray', *The Guardian*, 9 Feb. 1996, p.10.
19. See Kissinger (note 7) p.36.
20. Hans Bethe, 'The Treaty Betrayed', *The New York Review of Books*, 21 Oct. 1999.
21. 'A Foreign Policy for the Global Age', Official Text, Office of Public Affairs, US Embassy, London, 23 Oct. 2000.
22. 'Brittan in fierce attack on US trade policies', *Financial Times*, 22 May 1996.
23. 'West heads for trade war', *The Guardian*, 25 July 1996.
24. Nicole Gnesotto, 'An End to Introversion', *WEU Institute for Security Studies Newsletter* 34 (July 2001) p.1.
25. 'Europe Says US should Mend Fraying Alliance', *International Herald Tribune*, 24/25 Feb. 2001, p.1.
26. See Bierling (note 15) p.3.
27. It is no coincidence that the subject the British House of Commons Foreign Affairs Committee chose for its first inquiry in the new parliament elected in May 2001 was 'relations between the United Kingdom and the US and the implications of US foreign policy for UK interests'.
28. 'New Hope for the Old World', *Frankfurter Allgemeine Zeitung*, 20 Jan. 2001 (English Edition, 17/3) p.1.
29. 'Europe Says US should Mend Fraying Alliance' (note 25).
30. 'Master of the Universe', *The Guardian*, 7 Aug. 1996.

31. Henry Kissinger, 'At Sea in a New World', *Newsweek*, 6 June 1994, pp.6–8. See also Daniel Kaufman, David Clark and Kevin Sheehan (eds.) *US National Security Strategy for the 1990s* (Baltimore, MD: John Hopkins UP 1991).
32. Michael Cox, *US Foreign Policy After the Cold War: Superpower without a Mission?* (London: Pinter 1995) p.71.
33. See Kissinger (note 7) p.19.
34. For an analysis of structural change in transatlantic relations see Helga Haftendorn and Christian Tuschhoff (eds.) *America and Europe in an Era of Change* (Boulder, CO: Westview Press 1993) esp. Ch.1. See also Michael Winnerstig's neo-realist analysis of transatlantic security relations; *Shared Values or Power Politics? Transatlantic Security Relations 1981–94*, Research Report 26 (Stockholm: Swedish Inst. of Int. Affairs 1996).
35. See for example Margarita Mathiopoulos, 'Tripartite European Leadership and a New Trans-Atlantic Pact', *International Herald Tribune*, 29 March 2001.
36. Marc Grossman, 'US-European Partnership for the 21st Century', Official Text, Office of Public Affairs, US Embassy, 17 Sept. 1999, p.3.
37. This point is well made by Joseph Nye in *The Paradox of American Power: Why the World's Only Superpower Can't Go It Alone* (Oxford: OUP 2002).
38. See Daalder (note 13) p.564.
39. *The Economist*, 23 Oct. 1999, p.15.
40. See Ivo Daalder (note 13) p.559.
41. See Kissinger (note 7) p.82.

In Search of a New Role:
Poland in Euro-Atlantic Relations

OLAF OSICA

We want and we have to gain among the Allied states a position that will enable us to co-define de facto the Allied strategy and policies in a way that corresponds with our interests, particularly in Central and Eastern Europe. We have the potential to develop our human and economic resources and our pivotal strategic geographic location over the coming years into a position that will rank Poland among NATO's principal member states.

Foreign Minister Bronislaw Geremek in the Sejm on 9 April 1999

With its accession to NATO on 12 March 1999, Poland left behind it a history where its political roles hinged on the foreign policy gambles of its close neighbours. After 200 years of existence under limited or no sovereignty, Poland acquired a chance to become a meaningful actor in international politics. As Geremek has stated, joining NATO was perceived as a vital step in Poland's return to the role of a regional power. However, as it was soon discovered in Warsaw, transatlantic relations proved to be more diverse and less certain than their popular image in Poland had suggested.

Less than two weeks after Poland signed the Washington Treaty, the Alliance launched a military intervention in Kosovo, which put to the test the cohesion of NATO in particular and Euro-Atlantic relations in general. Moreover, conflicts that had swelled around the debates over the Common European Security and Defence Policy (CESDP) and Ballistic Missile Defense (BMD) come as surprises to Poland and wrecked a close-to-idyllic image in the Polish mind of transatlantic relations. As a result, Polish concerns over the future bonds of America and Europe, and particularly over the future of NATO have grown considerably.

Over the past three years, Poland has also faced a series of internal problems. In the absence of a coherent concept, and amid the worsening crisis of public finance and resistance from a part of the military, reform of the armed forces turned out to be a much more painful and intricate operation than was predicted when Poland was still applying for NATO membership. Amplifying that catalogue of surprises was the waning focus of NATO as an issue among Poland's political elites. While this had been strong during the membership application process, after 12 March 1999 the powerful political clout that Poland had mustered to expedite NATO enlargement either dissipated or was re-channelled into the accession negotiations with the European Union.

Against that backdrop, the September 2001 terrorist attacks on America and the subsequent US action in Afghanistan represent another and, possibly, the greatest challenge for Poland. Though their ultimate consequences are still hard to predict their impact is unlikely to leave thinking about the underlying principles of security relations between Europe, America and Russia unchanged, and will perhaps even alter the institutional shape of these relations. As it aspires to the position of an actor in the transatlantic relation, Poland, too, needs to undertake a fundamental review of the way it perceives its own security.

This article consists of two parts. The first is an overview of Polish security policy upon accession to NATO. It recounts Polish thinking on security and Euro-Atlantic relations, as well as the objectives that Poland intended to achieve through membership of NATO. The article highlights three aspects: the strong pro-Atlanticist stance; the incumbent internal thinking about Poland as a state, which in view of its history, neighbours' expectations and well-conceived self-interest, has an essential role to play in assuring security in Central and Eastern Europe (CEE). Another aspect in this discussion is the internal dynamics of Polish security policy.

The second part presents Poland as a nearly four-year-old participant in the Euro-Atlantic relations. It focuses on those aspects that reveal specific Polish interests and the way they have been articulated amidst strong external pressure for their re-definition. This analysis covers Polish views on the future of the Alliance, including its enlargement and the Polish attitude towards CESDP and BMD.

Overcoming Geopolitics

Europe's Weakness is America's Strength

Without detracting from the weight of many of the other motives that guided Poland in its accession to NATO, it can safely be stated that Poland's main political goal was to acquire the status of a United States ally. For Poland, it was because NATO's political and military attraction stemmed from its American leadership. That hackneyed phrase, shared by many European capitals, reflects in Poland's case something more than a rational political choice. It sets a *sui generis* paradigm for the Polish security policy, pre-determines the presence or absence of the sense of security within a prevailing majority of Poland's political elite, and conditions this elite's ability to face up to new challenges and rid itself of a psychological complex in its actions, particularly in its policy towards Russia.

Washington's power of influence on Polish policy is, on the one hand, the corollary of the military weakness and political indecision of European states. On the other hand, it is a function of the US political and military capabilities, which correspond with the traditional perception of security in Poland, that is security assured by force of arms and by the resolve to use it.

Though it is hard to comprehend, Polish politicians nurture a deep-rooted belief that, even if European states had the requisite capability for single-handed action, they would either not be prepared to employ it in Poland's defence, or their divergent interests would frustrate any effective single European operation. In other words, Poland's attitude towards Europe in security affairs is still being riddled with uncertainty, not to say mistrust. No doubt, this is to some extent a consequence of historical experience: the de facto refusal of France and Britain to rush to the relief of Poland in 1939, despite the existence of the mutual assistance treaties. Even if this 'complex of betrayal' by Europe is, arguably, fading, it still preys quite strongly on Polish minds.

It stems, in part, from the fact that, for the 45 years of the communist regime there was neither room nor climate in Poland to cope with that problem; in part also because the last 10 years of European policy towards Central-Eastern and Southern Europe provided further evidence that the lessons of history remain to be learned.

In the eyes of Polish politicians, the outbreak of war in the Balkans and the tragedy of Bosnia and Herzegovina lent further credibility to the idea that European powers care only about their own national interests. There was no one willing to die for Sarajevo, just as there had been no will to die for Gdansk. Similarly, the Polish political elite and society largely viewed European policy towards Russia as currying favour with Moscow at the expense of Warsaw, Vilnius or Kiev.

In this sense, close relations with the USA guarantee Poland's security, but also represent the strongest Polish foreign policy trump card[1] by essentially enhancing the value of Polish foreign policy in Europe. Inspired by the Anglo-American model, this belief grows from the idea of a 'strategic partnership' between Poland and the USA as a complement to the bilateral historical and cultural bonds, and sets the stage for joint activities in the region.

Washington effectively capitalises on those friendly sentiments and, aware of Poland's gratitude for NATO membership, gives Warsaw ample opportunity to show this gratitude in ways that benefit both countries. Examples of such activities include close cooperation between Polish and US special services dating back to the 1991 Persian Gulf War and the establishing afterwards (in the Polish Embassy in Baghdad) of an interest section representing the US.

Washington has also been supportive of Warsaw's political initiatives, such as the international conference 'Towards Community of Democracies'.[2]

Furthermore, after 11 September 2001, when the slow US acceptance of offers of military assistance sparked a debate about an American rebuff of its main allies, President George W. Bush made two essential gestures that brought Poland back on the European political scene. First, he arranged a video-conference on anti-terrorism with the participants of the CEE countries and later he requested Poland, as one of a limited group of NATO allies, to dispatch a contingent of soldiers to the Afghan operation.

Poland's political circles also remember that the Americans provided finance for the training of Poland's special troop GROM, the first to be fully interoperable with NATO. America is also handing over armaments to the Polish armed forces and is financing projects important to Poland, such as the Polish-American-Ukrainian Cooperation Initiative (PAUCI) and the Polish-Ukrainian battalion, which operates under the Stability Force in Bosnia.

Equally noteworthy is the political support that Washington has shown towards Poland, its history and the successes that have been achieved over the last decade. It is also a political support that is reciprocated, with American policy enjoying tremendous support from Polish public and political opinion alike.[3]

Poland's closeness to the US is the reason why the Warsaw's security policy is seen in Europe as obsessively pro-American and much less geared towards European interests as it is motivated by loyalty towards the transatlantic ally. Traditionally, Poland has dismissed that charge as both untrue and as a product of the rivalry between some French-led EU countries and the USA. In practice, however, the more strains appear in relations between Warsaw and Paris or Berlin (even if not immediately security-related, but concerning the Polish EU accession negotiations), the stronger in Polish policy runs the trend to stake all on Washington.

This is also accompanied by growing scepticism towards Europe and its new political projects. Poland's first reactions to the European Council decisions in Cologne and Helsinki on the development of CESDP are a clear illustration of these attitudes. Poland's sense of rejection by the EU, suspicion of Paris's intentions and concern that this project may give Russia a wholly unjustified handle on Europe's security prevailed over positive arguments.[4]

Another victim of the same development was the Weimar Triangle – a Polish-Franco-German initiative, originally designed as Poland's gateway to European affairs, including security – which provides a saddening illustration of the apathy that Poland's political dialogue with Germany and France is suffering from. Whereas Paris turned out to be a great heartbreak, with Poland failing to seduce France into working more closely together in European matters, the weakening of political cooperation with Germany began to show immediately after the decision on NATO's enlargement.

Surprisingly enough, these developments have occurred alongside excellent military collaboration, frequent reciprocal visits by Polish, German and French officers, as well as joint military exercises.

As the vision of a strong, resolved America and a weak, unreliable Europe is inscribed in Polish security policy, signs of possible changes in this picture are beginning to filter through to the Polish political elite. America's ambivalent attitude towards Europe,[5] a growing penchant for unilateral action, particularly evident after 11 September 2001; the drift towards a militarised thinking about global security, but also the propensity of the United States to scale down its military involvement in Europe, all incite concerns.

Also, Washington increasingly reproaches Warsaw, first, for not proceeding quickly enough with its reform of the armed forces, and second, for its procrastination in its armed procurement decisions, particularly as regards supersonic fighter aircraft. As David Dunn argues, the USA is less and less content with mere political support for its operations, if it fails to be backed up with a tangible military muscle.

'For Your Freedom and Ours' – Poland as a Regional Power
Another factor with a strong impact on the Polish foreign and security policy is its sense of a 'community of destinies' with nations, whose independence was also undermined in the wake of the post-war division of Europe. At the source of such emotions are both common history – Lithuania, Ukraine and Belarus – and the experience of tragedies, which, over the past 50 years, alternately affected the Hungarians (1956), the Czechoslovakians (1968), the Poles (1981), and, more recently, the Baltic nations (1990).

Support for Belarussian opposition groups, permission to establish a Chechen centre and local radio in Poland and many humanitarian aid campaigns for Chechnya best illustrate the 'fraternity and solidarity' invoked by the head of Polish diplomacy. A posture of silent advocacy for the nations suffering under undemocratic regimes or nations fighting for their right to self-determination also became evident during NATO operations in Kosovo. Poland's approval of NATO actions was first of all a manifestation of support for international order, whereby action in defence of human rights may sanction the infringement of the sovereignty of a state that is a notorious violator of these rights.[6]

Although the Alliance's actions vis-à-vis Serbia were contested by a relevant segment of Polish politicians, there was no doubt that the call to defend the Albanians against cleansing by the Serbian military was enough for the Polish government to secure the support of a majority of public opinion in Poland.

This strong sense of a 'community of destinies' with countries in the region goes hand in hand with the desire, in Polish policy, to exercise political leadership in the region and bring knowledge about Eastern Europe into NATO and the EU. Underpinning this idea is the conviction that Poland, on account of its history, its role in the overthrow of communism and successful systemic transition, is almost predestined to play such a role.[7]

This conviction reflects perfectly the mood and expectations of many Polish politicians, who perceived NATO membership as the first step towards a sweeping turnaround in the geopolitics of the whole of Central and Eastern Europe, with EU membership being the second. Still valid as part of this first step is, on one hand, the freeing of the region from Russia's neo-imperial influence, and, on the other hand, ending Russia's expansion by establishing a 'democratic cordon' of states east of Poland.

This concept assigns to Poland the role of an advocate of the interests of Lithuania, Belarus and Ukraine in Western Europe and also of a guide for those countries in the implementation of their internal reforms. It prompted Poland's involvement in, among other things, the NATO-Ukraine Charter, Polish-American-Ukrainian Cooperation Initiative (PAUCI) and the establishment of joint battalions – Polish-Ukrainian and Polish-Lithuanian, and, more recently, also a Polish-Czech-Slovak brigade.

Paradoxically, however, Poland's NATO membership also gradually ushered in an awareness in Warsaw that the hopes hitherto associated with an Eastern policy stood less and less chances of materialising, and that that policy needed re-thinking.[8] This is evidently the case, given that the possibilities of Polish political influence in the East ran into the barrier of internal situations in Ukraine and Belarus. For this reason, and also because of its strong intrinsic limitations, Poland finds it extremely difficult to influence meaningfully the direction of change in those two countries. Thus, Polish policy towards its eastern neighbours, except Lithuania, needs a precise redefinition of its feasible potential. These unfortunately do not seem to include any loosening up of the relations between Russia and the Commonwealth of Independent States (CIS).[9]

Another limitation of Poland's eastern policy stems from the awareness that decisions about a stronger involvement of the European Union or NATO in the region's security, not to mention the enlargement decisions for both, hinge on the main actors of these institutions and hence still escape Poland's influence. On the other hand, these enlargements represent the main substance of Poland's Eastern policy: short of tapping the capabilities of NATO and the EU, Poland will not be in a position to stabilise its neighbourhood in an enduring manner, nor to promote its interests.

This probably explains why, as part of Poland's position in the NATO forum and also in the discussion on the future of the EU, the issue of security exportation has always taken precedence over the consequences that this process would have on the functions and future shapes of both organisations. The corollary of this attitude is, among other things, the prevailing perception of the EU's 'stabilising factor' role for Europe through the prism of EU enlargement to the East, over the perception of the EU as a 'political power', with an essential role in international politics. This attitude engenders a serious political dilemma and also strains in relations with the EU states, particularly with France and Germany.[10]

Internal Problems

In the lead up to NATO membership, there was widespread support for the impressive diplomatic effort that Poland displayed to gain entry. Indeed from the mid-1990s there was consensus among all political forces in Poland in favour of accession, which was supported by opinion poll data which regularly registered at over 60 per cent. Hence, it is all the harder to explain a clear downswing after 12 March 1999 in interest in NATO affairs, its future and problems. In what seems like a recurring pattern, issues of transatlantic security or of Poland's presence in the Alliance, including armed forces reform, become the focus of political discussions only when the allies are at loggerheads or when NATO levels its criticism at Poland.[11]

The wait-and-see attitude that is so common among Polish politicians is responsible for the fact that the Polish policy is largely reactive, and hence late by comparison to the policies of its new allies the other partners. In fact Poland's particular susceptibility to changes in European politics should provoke the opposite response. Suffice it to recall that the new editions of two documents, fundamental to Poland's security (the security strategy and the defence doctrine), were adopted as late as one year after Poland's accession to NATO. Thus, while already an ally to Germany, for one whole year Poland formally retained a doctrine that admitted the likelihood of aggression coming from all directions, including the West.

The main culprit of such a state of affairs seems to be the strong presence of history in Poland's security policy. Since the very outset, Poland has interpreted its membership in NATO more in categories of redressing historical injustice than for building new foreign policy foundations. Thus, when on 12 March 1999 the wrongs were made good, 'NATO-mania' went out of fashion, and the attention of public opinion and politicians shifted to the problems of negotiations with the EU.

However, this immersion in history is not only harmful to Poland's perspective, it is also prevents Warsaw from getting to grips with its new geopolitical situation. The latter changed twice in a decade for Poland (after 1989 and after 1999), and may change again in the wake of 11 September 2001. In other words, Polish policy is still having problems in defining its *raison d'état* in an autonomous manner that would take account of the dynamics of international policy. Forty-five years of membership in the communist bloc, with the USSR as the sole strategic overlord brooking no opposition, has clearly left havoc in its wake.[12]

Not having a fully developed intellectual and institutional base to fall back on, Poland's security policy – as well as its broadly conceived defence capability – is not only internally incoherent - and hence hardly intelligible to the allies, but is also vulnerable to dynamic political changes within the Polish state. One perfect example of this is the fate of successive plans for reform of the armed forces, which were either bogged down in unrealistic financial assumptions or revamped to suit the balance of forces in government. Thus, despite having been four years in the Alliance, Poland simply lacks a long-range plan for the development of its armed forces. This in part results from discord among political and military elites over the fundamental strategic purposes of these forces,[13] but it also follows on from the failure to provide an orderly defence base in the form of a transparent distribution of competencies between the organs of the state. It also lacks adequate legal regulations.[14]

Between Europe and America: Poland as a New Actor in Euro-Atlantic Relations

In view of observations made thus far, it can be said that Poland's security policy is the result of historical experiences, unconcealed aspirations to be a real actor and not merely a participant in Euro-Atlantic relations, as well as of objective limitations contingent on the internal or international situation. The Polish vision of NATO's future provides an illustration of how these three factors are interrelated. This will also include Poland's attitude to the further enlargement of the Alliance, the Polish position on the development of CESDP, and on the BMD.

The Future of NATO

In his presentation to the Sejm[15] debate in April 1999 on Poland's contribution to the discussion of the new strategic concept, Foreign Minister Bronislaw Geremek declared Poland's desire to 'preserve the power of its Article 5, the power of a defence alliance that it has held for 50 years'.[16]

The continuing attachment to NATO's traditional mission of collective defence has never signified opposition or reluctance to accept the Alliance's operations out of the area laid down in the Washington Treaty, in which Poland has always participated actively, garnering praise from the NATO Headquarters. Neither does it indicate blindness to the fact that, in the new geopolitical situation since 1989, Article 5 no longer constitutes as strong a foundation as it did during the Cold War. The emphasis on Article 5 stems from two assumptions.

First, in view of its geographic location (bordering Russia (Kaliningrad) and Belarus), Poland has a continued interest in preserving the traditional understanding of collective defence, that is, defence of the territory of the allied states. The mistrust of Russia, which from the outset treated NATO enlargement as a political attack on its sphere of influence, has continued. Indeed Russia's military build up in Kaliningrad and in Belarus, has further impeded any change in the Polish perception of security, which the elites still perceive through the prism of military force.[17]

Second, attachment to Article 5 is of essential political significance to Poland, because Poland regards collective defence as the pillar of internal stability amongst the Allies and the safeguard of their political equality vis-à-vis one another. As the fear of exclusion has been, and continues to be, Poland's foreign policy nightmare, being treated on a par with the old allies largely predetermines the sense of stability and hence security of Poland. It was for this reason that, when Poland was applying for membership, so much emphasis was placed on making sure that there would be no 'second class' membership for the new allies. Poland was keen to avoid any diluted status resulting from a formal and/or legally effective obligation by NATO to desist from the deployment of nuclear arms or troops on the territory of the new Members.

Poland's special attention to NATO's cohesion and political credibility also surfaced in the objection to the German Foreign Minister Joschka Fischer's proposal for NATO to unilaterally give up a potential first use of nuclear weapons.[18]

Not surprisingly, after the events of 11 September 2001, Poland re-emerged among the first-line allies, who not only rushed to declare unqualified assistance to the USA, but also supported recourse by the North Atlantic Council to Article 5 of the Washington Treaty, recognising this as a reaffirmation of the Alliance's strength and resilience.

The treatment of NATO as an 'exclusive club of equals', united around the objective of collective defence, is consequential in the perception of NATO's political activity towards third countries, particularly towards Russia. Poland supports, and is actively taking part in such cooperation, which does not at all detract from the Alliance's political autonomy, namely in the processes of Partnership for Peace, Membership Plan or NATO-Ukraine Commission.

However, the establishment of a NATO-Russia Permanent Joint Council met with scepticism. Poland considered the Foundation Act as providing Russia de facto with the possibility of intervening in allied operations. The Polish caution towards the strengthening of relations with Russia also resurfaced after 11 September, when 'in reward' for active support for the anti-terrorist coalition, the NATO Secretary-General suggested that the dialogue with Russia be elevated to a 'qualitatively higher level'.[19] As Minister for Foreign Affairs, Cimoszewicz, stated it 'would be very important to develop this NATO-Russia cooperation in practice and then align institutional solutions to it, rather than doing it in a reverse sequence'.[20]

With, or Without the Mandate?

One interesting feature of Poland's vision of NATO's role is the Polish attitude to 'out-of-area' operations, and particularly NATO's legitimacy for conducting them. The issue arose in the discussion on the legality of the Alliance's intervention in Kosovo. In that debate, Poland let itself be known as an ally, for whom the lack of solid legal basis was no obstacle to allied operations. Although the political elites concurred that the situation was not ideal, they also believed that where human rights were at stake, their defence should take precedence over the sovereignty of a state.[21]

Elucidating his government's position on the Balkan intervention, Minister Geremek made no bones about the fact that

> ...the best way to do it is when a mandate for such missions is issued by the Security Council on behalf of the United Nations. At the same time, however (...) given the entire veto technology in the Security Council, one must not make NATO's moves contingent on the votes of either Russia or China, or both, and that NATO's missions going beyond Article 5 in emergencies may be pursued by NATO when they are consistent with the principles of the United Nations Charter and are in the service of the values enshrined therein.

And these values are the human rights, the universal character of which is – as the Minister said – the foundation of Poland's foreign policy. Although the statement by Geremek mirrored the views of the government and parliamentary majority, it would be wrong to assume that the Polish political elites were of one mind as to the rationale behind and legitimacy of the Kosovo operation. Critical voices and biased reports on the Allied operation, partial disclosures of only the Kosovar tragedies, while dwarfing the Serbian ones, and also voices critical of the missing legal basis for the whole operation were not unusual at this time. Many politicians were openly critical of these policies, particularly those from the two main opposition parties at that time – the SLD (Democratic Left's Alliance) and the PSL (Polish People's Party with a largely rural electorate).

Public opinion surveys also reveal that support for military operations involving Polish soldiers is not granted automatically. Support for the involvement of Polish troops in Bosnia and Kosovo was indeed quite strong (respectively 35 per cent[22] and 32 per cent[23]), but it never reached 50 per cent. It should also be borne in mind that so far Polish forces have not been involved in regular war that came with the first phase of the Kosovo operation, but only in peacekeeping missions. That the public opinion in Poland is not prepared to accept any kind of armed force engagement is also attested to by surveys on the support for Polish troop involvement in the Afghan operation. In October 2001, 64.7 per cent of the respondents were against, whereas 28.1 per cent were in favour.[24] In January 2002, the support increased to 43 per cent, with the same percentage of objecting respondents.[25]

NATO's Enlargement

There is arguably no country in the Alliance that cares more about the second round of NATO's enlargement than Poland. The admission of new members is much more important to Poland than the implementation of other political projects such as CESDP or BMD. When the Polish press was reeling from the news that, in return for the Russian consent to renegotiations of the Anti-Ballistic Missile Treaty (ABM) and hence to the deployment by the USA of the missile defence system, Washington would be prepared to give up or postpone the second enlargement of NATO, President Kwasniewski declared outright that 'from the Polish point of view, the enlargement of NATO is the priority, because the prospect of a stray missile from an exotic country striking at Poland is much in the sphere of theory'.[26]

Support for NATO enlargement is based on three premises.

First, it answers the security needs of the CEE countries, which Poland also recognises perfectly well.

Second, it represents another step in overcoming the geopolitics of a region that still feels itself crouching under the shadow of Russia's politics. This, in turn, as well as the criteria that the applicant countries have to comply with, firmly reinforces and stabilises Poland's position, as the questions of regional security thereby transcend the Euro-Atlantic framework.

And finally, NATO enlargement, especially if it follows Polish expectations, increases the potential to further Polish interests in the region and consolidates the US presence in Europe in general. Hence, although Polish diplomacy officially supports the aspirations of all states applying for membership in the Alliance, in reality only the membership of Slovakia and at least one Baltic state – Lithuania – is of political relevance.

Although enlargement is of utmost importance to Poland and is a policy which generates consensual support among the Polish elite, there is also an acute awareness of some of the potential dilemmas for NATO that enlargement presents.[27] The most obvious of these is the problem that the admission of new members will not amplify NATO's military capabilities, while expanding the area of its responsibility. Furthermore, the admission of new members will signify a further internal differentiation within the Alliance. The new members will not only bring in their own interests and their specific perceptions of security, but also their different political cultures. Remembering that the different perception of threats and the different views on how to prevent them became at one time the bone of contention between Europe and America, enlargement may do more damage to NATO's political cohesion and capability for effective action.

From Poland's point of view, the most important thing is for the new members to be politically reliable allies, who will not contest allied decisions and erode the political cohesion of the organisation, as Czech policy did during the NATO intervention in Kosovo.

The issue of the candidates' military capabilities has never figured on the front burner in Poland, and, recently, has even been pushed to the back one. First, it could become an obstacle to the admission of new states and, second, due to the delays in implementing the objectives agreed with NATO, Polish politicians and diplomats find it awkward to raise this question in the international forum. Poland's concern over the candidates' military capabilities is evident mainly in the shared experiences of Poland's integration with the Alliance, supplemented at times by armament handovers to these candidates.

Between Defence Policy and Missile Defence

Quite unexpectedly, the discussions on CESDP and on BMD became, to varying degrees and with different consequences, a test of Poland's ability to pursue an active policy as a NATO member state. As Warsaw saw it, from the very outset neither project seemed to be worth the problems that they caused in the Euro-Atlantic relations. And besides, in contrast to NATO's further enlargement, neither was a central concern of Polish security policy. That was why, in evaluating both projects, Poland paid more attention to their potential impact on Euro-Atlantic relations than to their actual content.[28]

Poland harboured the most serious doubts and reservations about the concept of CESDP,[29] which, unlike the vague 'protective shield' concept, was of immediate significance to the effectiveness of the Alliance, as well as the role and place of the USA in crisis management in Europe. Thus, when the EU resolved in Cologne (June 1999) and six months later in Helsinki, to establish its own Rapid Reaction Forces and crisis management mechanisms, Warsaw clearly outlined its interests and expectations. This position can be seen from two standpoints.

The first concerns the Polish vision of the EU's future and hence the question of the rationale behind the development of a European defence policy. It would not be an overstatement to say that that concept did not always meet with understanding in Warsaw. First, Polish politicians believed that the best place to develop European capabilities in defence policy was within NATO and, more specifically, within the context of the alliance's European Security and Defence Identity (ESDI) that had been developing since the mid-1990s. It enabled the European allies to take action without American participation, but did not usher in the political and institutional competition that had begun to develop between NATO and the EU since the birth of CESDP. In effect, Poland, as a NATO member and a candidate to the EU, found itself formally outside CESDP, which had a huge impact on Poland's perception of that concept.

But the difficulty of accepting CESDP was also the corollary of Poland's perception of the European integration process: through the prism of a delayed decision on enlargement of the Union rather than of decisions to build a 'political union' with effective foreign and defence policies as part of it. Accompanying this was considerable doubt as to whether the EU states could overcome their military impotence in the foreseeable future. Rather, Poland suspected that CESDP would remain 'a paper tiger', which would only substantially complicate relations within NATO and hence between Europe and the USA. Although the aforesaid elements concerned more the background to the Polish discussion about the sense or nonsense of a European defence policy, than the intrinsic merit of the CESDP concept, they weighed heavily on Poland's official position and how it was presented.

That position referred almost exclusively to the principles behind the creation and future operation of CESDP, and, above all, the relations between the EU and NATO, and between the EU and the so-called 'Six' non-EU European members of NATO: Poland, Czech Republic, Hungary, Norway, Turkey and Iceland.[30]

In his address at the University of Warsaw in May 2001, Foreign Minister Wladyslaw Bartoszewski stated that 'the EU-established principles of the EU relations with third states, particularly NATO members and candidates to the EU do not factually assure the possibilities of cooperation with respect to CESDP. Consultations and dialogue will not substitute for real cooperation.'[31] The head of Polish diplomacy also listed numerous detailed questions to which, in his view, clear answers were still missing. Included in these were:

> ...a) the definition, following the NATO pattern, of a European strategic concept; b) answer to the question as to where – in geographic sense – the EU intended to use its forces; c) in what specific situations; d) how the EU military operations will be conducted; e) what should be the scope of military planning and training; f) how in practice decisions will be made with regard to a specific crisis management response; g) what should be the relationship between the Common Foreign and Security Policy (The EU's second pillar)and the fully developed ESDP.

These views of the head of Polish diplomacy still inform Poland's standpoint on CESDP. Moreover, this remains the case even though the

British-brokered 'Ankara Covenant' on the principles of relations between the 'Six' and the EU, met with a very positive response from Poland because it addresses all the concerns that Poland had raised earlier. The agreement broke Turkey's resistance to allowing the EU permanent and guaranteed access to the NATO assets and capabilities, and to the talks on the rules underpinning EU cooperation with the Alliance. However, following an objection by Greece, the agreement was not adopted by the European Council at the Laeken Summit and now, after two years of talks between the EU and NATO and the EU and the 'Six', progress remains modest.

In contrast to the CESDP concept, the BMD project did not elicit major interest and concern on the part of Polish politicians. Since Washington's plans triggered many controversies both within NATO and in relations with Russia, Warsaw, like most European capitals, was watching the whole discussion from the sidelines and was in no hurry to adopt an official position.

This approach did not change until 2001, and when it did, it did not originate in the Foreign Ministry, but in the National Security Council (RBN) of the Polish President. The communiqué on the RBN session of 22 February, presented orally by Minister Siwiec, included the statement that,

> ...it is in Poland's interest to see what originally was called the national missile defence system become a system that also applies to the allies, a system that will afford more security to the NATO members and co-operating countries, and will not lead to new threats. We are interested in this dialogue to be held in the forum of the North Atlantic Alliance and in furnishing appropriate conditions for talks with Russia and other countries that voice doubts about the expediency of this system.

Siwiec also noted that BMD could not itself replace in a simple and technological way the security provided by the prevailing strategic arms reduction regimes and arms control in general.[32]

After a few months, during which no relevant developments took place either on the BMD issue or in the Polish debate over that concept, another statement was made. Again its source was not the Foreign Ministry but the General Staff of the Polish Armed Forces in the person of the Chief of Staff, General Piatas. He told the session of the NATO Chiefs of Staff in May 2001 that elements of the BMD, such as launch pads or radars, could be deployed on Poland's territory and that Poland would even be prepared to share in the costs of some systems required by the defence systems. The

General was backed by Defence Minister Komorowski, who pointed out that the scourge of history – Poland's geopolitical location – was turning into an asset in the construction of BMD, because Poland's territory and defence system were thus becoming part of the common missile defence structure.[33]

In view of the fact that there were no NATO military installations or command structures in Poland,[34] the deployment in Poland of the system elements would strengthen Poland's importance for NATO.[35]

However, the reaction of foreign ministry officials to what General Piatas had said left no room for doubt that his declaration was firmly premature. Although Deputy Foreign Minister Meller admitted that Poland was 'vitally interested in the concept and was attentively watching its evolution', support was limited to exploratory discussions and that Poland was not yet at a stage that would make its technical involvement in the project a foregone conclusion.[36]

A few weeks after the Chief of Staff's speech, it was clearly apparent that both the General Staff and Ministry of Defence had jumped the gun and that the opinion of the Foreign Ministry would eventually prevail. At the meeting of NATO defence ministers in June 2001, Minister Komorowski spoke only of 'understanding for the other parties' concerns', and stressed that the interests of all the allies should be taken into account in the implementation of the shield concept and that the idea itself should not infringe on the architecture of European security.

Summary

Due to its geographical situation and its historical experiences, Poland's efforts to join NATO were mainly motivated by the disposition to become, first of all, a consumer of security offered by the Alliance. This disposition continues to shape the thinking of Polish politicians, who attach greater weight to the preservation of those NATO functions that safeguard defence than to those that could make NATO an instrument of Polish foreign policy.

The difficulty of switching to the role of 'security provider' which the allies clearly expect of Poland, primarily stems from Poland's perception of a continuing Russian threat. Suspicion of the motives behind the Russian policy, which is trying to mark its political presence in the region in ways that do not always converge with the interests of nations inhabiting it, colours Poland's perception of international politics. For Warsaw, it is a tough game of national interests where success only comes to those states that have political power based on military strength. This 'neorealist' perspective makes it imperative, on the one hand, to think about security in the traditional manner, and, on the other hand, to approach with caution those efforts that aim to embed Europe's security in a system of cooperative security[37] or of European guarantees.

Without Russia's full democratisation and the solidification of Poland's position in NATO, and subsequently in the EU, no radical turn-around in the Polish reasoning on security appears possible. The awareness that this reasoning is largely divorced from the challenges being faced by Poland's main allies in NATO cannot of itself initiate a change. The resulting divergence between Poland's political ambitions and the potential of the Polish state, lie at the heart of Polish security policy.

A further dichotomy also exists there between the past, with the concomitant need to partake in NATO's strong exclusive club mainly caring for its members, and the present, with the concomitant need to engage Poland's capabilities for the security of third nations. This gives rise to a conflict of two visions: of Poland as a 'security consumer' and of Poland as a 'security provider'. This conflict not only makes its impossible for Poland to define its role in NATO, but also engenders problems in Poland's political activity and reform of the armed forces.

It is also standing in the way of Poland's involvement in CESDP which, with its emphasis on expeditionary capabilities, is regarded as a competitive bid vis-à-vis the objectives of NATO that are also about the traditional defence capabilities.

Meanwhile, the simple reserves, through which Poland became politically integrated with the Alliance and supported its operations in the Balkans, are running out. Short of a profound reassessment of the threats to its security and the role of its armed forces, Poland will face reduced room for manoeuvre for working together with the allies. In this sense, Poland's real, not just declarative, participation in the implementation of the Defence Capabilities Initiative as well as the European Headline Goal is of fundamental importance, as both projects are like a registration fee for a serious political game.

Paying that fee opens up the long-term prospect of a real co-shaping of NATO and EU policies. Not paying it mercilessly relegates Poland to the role of a bystander to the policy mainstream of both organisations. Speeding up reform of the armed forces is all the more important given that, since 11 September 2001, thinking about the nature of allied military operations is subject to change. Select coalitions of states who are willing to act and who command relevant military capabilities will replace the joint 'contributory' missions. Thus, the total of 275 troops that Poland has

declared for operations in Afghanistan may, in future, turn out to be a
shortfall that will not justify the demand for equal treatment with the
other allies.

NOTES

1. Foreign Minister Wladyslaw Bartoszewski's speech in the Sejm, 6 April 2001.
2. The conference was held 26–27 June 2000. See *Polish Quarterly of International Affairs 2* (Spring 2000) pp.5–63.
3. President George W. Bush's 'Address to Faculty and Students of Warsaw University', Office of the Press Secretary, 15 June 2001.
4. O. Osica, 'CESDP as Seen by Poland', *Reports & Analyses 5/01* (Warsaw: Center for International Relations 2001) <www.csm.org.pl/english>.
5. B. Geremek, 'Najwazniejsze pytania: miedzy poezja a ksiegowoscia', *Unia&Polska*, 18 June 2001.
6. B. Geremek, 'Sovereignty and Human Rights: United Nations in the 21st Century', *Polish Quarterly of International Affairs* 4 (Winter 1999) pp.5–15.
7. *Rzeczpospolita*, 16 Feb. 1999.
8. One manifestation of this reflection was a series of articles published in *Tygodnik Powszechny* and touched off by another article by B. Sienkiewicz, 'Pochwala minimalizmu' *(Praise of Minimalism)* (TP 52/53 2000), which then set the stage for a discussion forum at the Stefan Batory Foundation. The transcript of that discussion is available on the Foundation's website <www.batory.org.pl>.
9. See Sienkiewicz (note 8).
10. 'Europa mit dreissig und mehr Mitgliedern', Joint document by the planning staffs of the German and French foreign ministries, Nov. 1998–June 2000.
11. Address by the NATO Secretary-General, Lord Robertson, 'European Security in the 21st Century – Completing Europe's Unfinished Business', University of Warsaw, 29 March 2001.
12. B. Balcerowicz, 'Armed forces in Polish Defense Policy', in R. Kuzniar *et al.* (eds.) *Poland's Security Policy* (New Delhi: Scholar 2001) pp.439–66.
13. In spite of the reform plan, which is the basis for reform in 2001–2006, there still exists in Poland a split between the advocates of a small, but all professional, state-of-the-art Army, which would mainly participate in NATO's out-of-area operations, and the advocates of preserving conscription and holding strong ground forces, which would first of all defend Poland against external aggression.
14. See M. Likowski, 'Balagan prawny grozniejszy niz slaba armia (Legal mess is more dangerous than a weak army)', *Raport WTO* 10 (2001) pp.4–7.
15. Lower chamber of the Polish parliament.
16. During the debate over the directions of Polish foreign policy – see the transcript of the Sejm session on 8 April 1999.
17. In the period preceding the formal accession to NATO, the scene of such actions were the Vienna negotiations on adapting the CFE Treaty reduction agreement signed way back in 1990. See *Rzeczpospolita*, 9 Dec. 1998. For more on the subject, see A. Kobieracki, 'Problem of Disarmament in Poland's Security Policy', in Kuzniar *et al.* (note 12) pp.389–417.
18. *Rzeczpospolita*, 9 Dec. 1998.
19. *Rzeczpospolita*, 23 Dec. 2001.
20. Quoted from PAP report, 26 Nov. 2001. The head of BBN, Minister Siwiec, stated, on the other hand, during his visit to Russia that the NATO-Russia relations should rest on the principle of '*so much co-decision as much co-responsibility*'. Quoted from PAP report, 27 Nov. 2001.
21. Sejm debate on the directions of Polish foreign policy on 8 April 1999.
22. CBOS opinion poll in Sept. 1995.
23. CBOS opinion poll in April 1999.

24. *Rzeczpospolita*, 23 Nov. 2001. Opinion poll held 27–28 Oct. 2001.
25. But as many as 68 per cent of the respondents said that NATO's action in Afghanistan was justified. CBOS opinion poll on 10–14 Jan. 2002, quoted after PAP report, 29 Jan. 2002.
26. *Gazeta Wyborcza*, 21 June 2001.
27. Valuable material for thought is found in the Euro-Atlantic Association's report entitled 'Rozszerzenie NATO' (The Enlargement of NATO), Warsaw (March 2000).
28. PAP press agency report, 13 June 2001.
29. For a detailed description of Poland's stance on CESDP and its evolution in the period between June 1999 and June 2001 see Osica (note 4).
30. See H. Szlajfer, 'Kszta_towanie europejskiej polityki bezpieczenstwa i obrony: polska perspektywa' (The shaping of European security and defence policy), *Rocznik Strategiczny 1999/2000* (Strategic Yearbook) pp.33–4.
31. W. Bartoszewski, 'European Security Policy – A Polish View' in J. Barcz and K. Zukrowska (eds.) *The Future of the European Union – A Polish View* (Warsaw 2001) pp.76–90.
32. See communiqué on the RBN session of 22 Feb. 2000, <www.bbn.gov.pl>.
33. See *Polska Zbrojna* 22 (2001) p.33.
34. Officially, the Szczecin-based Polish-German-Danish 'Nord-East' corps is not subordinated to NATO.
35. See *Gazeta Wyborcza*, 17 July 2001.
36. See *Polska Zbrojna*, 22 (2001) p.33.
37. J. Czaputowicz, *System czy nielad?* (A system or disorder?) (Warsaw 1998) p.223. See also remarks of Foreign Minister B. Geremek in *Common strategy towards Ukraine?* (Warsaw: Center for International Relations 1999) p.27.

Modernizing the Polish Military

ANDREW A. MICHTA

Poland inherited from the communist era the largest non-Soviet military establishment of the Warsaw Pact. Approximately 400,000 strong, the Polish People's Army was a draftee-based officer-heavy behemoth, structured and trained for offensive operations against NATO. Its officer corps had a strong sense of professional pride and duty to the nation. However, its reputation was tainted by a pattern of intervention in domestic politics, including the suppression of the Solidarity movement in 1981.

Reforming the Polish armed forces in preparation for NATO membership was a daunting task. As the government moved to rebuild democratic institutions and to reform the economy, the defense ministry tried to contain excessive personnel costs, establish a Western pattern of civil-military relations, reduce military bases heavily concentrated in the western part of the country, and maintain the largely obsolescent Soviet-era equipment.

Personnel reductions would prove difficult and costly. For example, in 1989 the Land Forces (the core of the Polish military) numbered 310,000 personnel, which the defense budget simply could no longer support.[1] The numbers tell only a part of the story; equally troubling was the structure of the force. The communist-era Polish People's Army was an 'army of colonels', with a staffing pattern reminiscent of an inverted pyramid: top-heavy and lacking a professional NCO corps. The historical pattern of civil-military relations would prove a major obstacle to reform when Polish military tradition collided with NATO requirements. Equipment issues were equally pressing, especially the need to modernize communication and control systems and obsolete aircraft. Though rudimentary compatibility with NATO would eventually be achieved, equipment modernization remains a burning issue.

Since 1999 it has become apparent where Polish military reform has succeeded and where problems remain. This article will briefly review the record of institutional reform leading up to Poland's membership in

NATO, with an emphasis on force reductions and a new pattern of civil-military relations. It will then focus on the most urgent current task of equipment modernization, taking as the baseline the 2001–2006 program. It will conclude with a brief assessment of Poland's performance as a NATO ally.

Downsizing and Civil-Military Relations

In order to create a Western-style military, the Polish defense ministry needed to reduce the size of the armed forces, restructure the institutions, and modernize the equipment. It became clear early on in the process that most of the effort would focus on the first two objectives, while equipment modernization would be limited to achieving rudimentary interoperability and compatibility with NATO.[2]

The pain of radical downsizing was felt across the spectrum of the Polish military establishment. By 1999 the armed forces were cut down to half of their former numerical strength. Already in 1995, the land forces were reduced to 158,400, the air and air defense forces to 73,100, and the navy to 19,700.[3] Such drastic cuts had an impact not only on the careers of individual officers, but also on entire communities where troops were stationed. Personnel reductions and the closing of military installations hit communities hard, especially as the defense ministry moved to alter the Soviet-era deployment pattern.

In the late 1980s the bulk of Polish operational forces was concentrated in the western part of the country. In keeping with the Warsaw Pact era strategy, 60 per cent of military assets were located in western Poland, 30 per cent in the center, and only 10 per cent in the east. By 1995 the defense ministry managed to partially redeploy the forces to bring about a more balanced defense of national territory, with the deployment of 40 per cent in the west, 30 per cent in the centre and 30 per cent in the east (at the time Poland added a fourth military district). This redeployment pattern would be reviewed yet again, and it would subsequently be modified in preparation for NATO membership.

At the heart of the institutional reform was a change in the military's 'corporate culture' that would bring Poland in line with NATO first and foremost and with respect to the core issues of civilian control over the military, budgeting and planning methods. The politics of Polish defense reform were entangled in the country's systemic transformation after four decades of communist rule. It was also a part of the larger question about coming to terms with the historically established military ethos especially in the area of civil-military relations and parliamentary oversight.

As articulated by Jeffrey Simon, the Western norm of civil-military relations included (1) a clear division of authority between the president and the government (prime minister and defense/interior minister) in the constitutions or through public law; (2) parliamentary oversight of the military through control of the defense budgets; (3) peacetime government oversight of general staffs and military commanders through civilian defense ministries; and (4) restoration of military prestige, trustworthiness, and accountability for the armed forces to be effective.[4]

The Western norm was applied against the backdrop of the Polish military's historical experience of intervention in domestic politics. In the interwar period the army played a dominant role in Poland, as both the progenitor of independence and the controlling force after the 1926 coup led by Marshal Jozef Pilsudski. During the communist era, the military was the ultimate domestic guarantor of the communist system, while at the same time it played an important role in the succession of internal crises, beginning with the 1956 Polish October, through the 1970 and 1976 crises, and culminating in the 1981 martial law that suppressed the Solidarity movement.

The communist-era civil-military relations resulted in a senior officer corps with little exposure to strategic planning and security policymaking, and with no experience in democratic civil-military relations and parliamentary oversight. Highly patriotic, Polish officers understood civilian control as the government's prerogative to use the armed forces for political purposes at home. Based on its experience under communism, the senior officer corps now defined professionalism as a broad autonomy for the military within the structure of the state. While they shared the national aspirations of the citizenry to a sovereign and democratic state, they mistrusted the civilians.[5] Conversely, the early Solidarity-based governments had a bitter memory of the army's role in 1981 and of the subsequent martial law regime.

The lessons on civil-military relations that the military had drawn from the communist experience were startling: between 1991 and 1995 the Polish general staff sought to insulate itself from civilian oversight in the defence ministry and at the parliamentary level, seeking instead direct subordination of the military to the authority of the president. Instead of building an institution-based framework of civil-military relations, Poland drifted during the early transition period toward an arrangement increasingly based on patronage and personal loyalties.

The period was marked by a deepening crisis in civil-military relations that threatened to decouple the military and civilian authorities. As they sought to bypass the defence minister, President Lech Walesa and General

Tadeusz Wilecki, the Chief of the General Staff, developed a formula that would subordinate the chief of the general staff directly to the president. A series of confrontations between Walesa and several defense ministers moved Poland dangerously close to a constitutional crisis and jeopardized the country's prospects for membership of NATO. The crisis generated considerable concern in Brussels and Washington, and led to pressure from NATO to reverse course.

A breakthrough in civil-military relations in Poland came after the 1995 election of Aleksander Kwasniewski, a former communist, as Poland's president. Kwasniewski signed the new 'Law on the Office of the Defence Minister' that subordinated the general staff to the defence minister. The final chapter of the struggle over the institutional framework of civil-military relations in Poland came with the passage of the new 'large constitution', adopted by the National Assembly on 2 April 1997 and approved in a referendum on 25 May 1997. Article 134 of the new basic law reaffirms the presidential prerogative, but it also makes the defence minister the direct superior of the armed forces in peacetime.

The resolution of the crisis in civil-military relations allowed Poland to accelerate the process of institutional transformation in preparation for NATO membership. The time between NATO's 1997 decision to invite Poland to join and the country's formal accession to the alliance in 1999 was a period of intensive work and rapid organizational adjustment. After the invitation to Poland to join NATO was issued, the Partnership for Peace (PfP) standards were rapidly replaced with NATO norms. After 1997 Poland worked to implement 67 classified goals that focused on interoperability at the level of a NATO ally. During the successive rounds of accession talks, the Poles had to meet legal reforms and military criteria, make specific financial commitments, and implement NATO procedural requirements. This was accompanied by the modernization of selected airfields and harbors to meet basic interoperability requirements.

Most importantly, as Poland neared NATO membership, it continued the process of depoliticising its military through the implementation of a new legal framework and through further personnel reductions. The reorganization of the defence ministry continued into 2002; the most recent changes that came into effect in January that year eliminated close to 200 jobs and offered early retirement to 700 senior officers.

Finally, a generational shift began to make its mark, as younger officers with experience in NATO structures were promoted and began to exercise leadership. After a decade of often contentious reform and four years into its membership in NATO, the Polish military is structured in key areas in accordance with NATO standards.

Equipment Modernization, 2001–2006

While Poland has achieved considerable success transforming its civil-military relations and restructuring its military institutions, equipment modernization remains a work in progress and a cause for concern in Brussels. A serious effort to address the hardware and readiness problems only came after 1999, when the issue was framed not just in terms of interoperability and compatibility between the Polish armed forces and NATO, but increasingly in terms of Poland's contribution to NATO missions commensurate with its potential as an ally.

Today, equipment modernization is the number one priority of the defence ministry. Not only is it essential to the country's ability to discharge its obligations to the alliance, but it also affects Poland's standing in NATO and it drives the professionalization of the military. In the final analysis, no amount of institutional structural change will suffice if the soldiers are not given the tools to do their job.

Poland has had more than its share of partly implemented and aborted military modernization plans. The current 2001–2006 modernization program, adopted in January 2001, holds the most promise, as it spells out a five-year sustained government commitment to defense. It promises 1.95 per cent of the country's gross domestic product for defence over the program's duration. It targets the armed forces for further reductions, down to 150,000 personnel overall, to be accompanied by the closing of 40 military bases, cutting the number of military academies from eight to five, a 40 per cent reduction in infrastructure (barracks, depots, training grounds), and the withdrawal from service of the oldest ships, all MiG-21 aircraft and all T-55 tanks. Poland will also withdraw from service its 152mm and 122mm howitzers, as it introduces the NATO compatible 'Chrobry' system.

The program stipulates a further reduction of the officer corps by 6,000–7,000. The program should realize a saving of 6 billion zlotys.[6] More importantly, the government promised that the share of the budget spent on modernization would rise from about 12 per cent now to 23 per cent by 2006.[7] In an effort to free additional resources for new equipment in 2002, the defence ministry has decided not to call up 18,000 draftees scheduled for basic training and 2,750 college graduates scheduled for officer courses, which should yield savings of approximately 200 million zlotys.[8]

Equipment modernization requires better-trained personnel to handle the new hardware, and as such, it is an integral part of the increased professionalization of the Polish military. The introduction of Western weapon systems has a spillover effect on training and retention, as well as on the overall skill level of personnel. These are the reasons why, in addition to the weapon systems themselves, the acquisition of NATO technology is so important to the overall quality of the Polish armed forces.

The defence ministry's shopping list is long. Priority items include a new wheeled personnel carrier, airlift capability, continued modernization of communication systems, and a multi-purpose fighter aircraft. The acquisition of transport aircraft is essential for Poland's participation in NATO missions. The Polish force deployed to Afghanistan in March 2002 was transported on two Ukrainian Antonov-124 transports because Poland had none.

The purchase of a new fighter aircraft is another difficult issue, framed by both budgetary and political constraints. The impending choice by the defence ministry between the US F-16, the Swedish JAS Gripen, and French Mirage-2000, expected this winter, will have a lasting impact, not only on the development of the air force, but also on several ancillary issues, including Poland's future major contracts and the country's eventual participation in the Joint Strike Fighter program. In the meantime, the air force has tried to make do with the legacy systems. The recent agreement to transfer 23 additional MiG-29 aircraft from Germany (purchased for the symbolic price of 1 euro), will help with training and spare parts; however, it will not solve the critical issue of supplying the air force with a modern multi-purpose aircraft.

Given the dearth of funds, equipment modernization in Poland has been a mixture of planned acquisitions and transfers of surplus equipment from allied governments. The latter can play a significant role in accelerating change within the Polish military, as well as opening up new opportunities for Poland's cash strapped defense industry. The transfer of 128 Leopard 2 A4 tanks from Germany to equip the 10th Armored Cavalry Brigade at Swietoszow, though not central to Polish military modernization, has been an important step in the direction of ensuring interoperability with NATO. It illustrates the impact Western technology can have on the overall modernization of the Polish armed forces and the restructuring of the country's defense industry.

The cost of the Leopard 2 transfer is small compared to the value of the German equipment: the Poles will pay 25 million euros to acquire the tanks. The delivery of the Leopards will be completed by the end of this year. The 2001–2006 hardware modernization program stipulates the withdrawal from service of all remaining T-55 tanks, which should leave the Polish armed forces with some 850 T-72 and PT-91 'Twardy' tanks in service. The acquisition of the German tank may allow for further reductions without giving up the overall capability, as the Leopard's performance exceeds the parameters of the T-series platform. It is likely that once the transfer of the Leopard 2 has been completed, Poland can bring down the overall size of its tank force to 500, releasing additional funds from maintenance for modernization.

The transfer of German tanks should also allow Polish tank crews to move their training forward by one generation of equipment, especially in the area of fire control which on Leopard 2 exceeds the parameters of Polish systems to date. The transfer of German tanks to Poland should also mark the beginning of cooperation between Polish and German armor manufacturers, because the introduction of German main battle tanks will require cooperation in the area of ammunition manufacturing, maintenance and support. With proper budgeting, German technology can have an impact on the remaining legacy systems that require modernization in the coming years. Finally, the introduction of the Leopard will push Poland further toward professionalization, as support for the German tank demands skill levels and experience that exceed those of an average draftee. In the long run, the defence ministry could realize additional savings on maintenance, because the cost of maintaining the Leopard 2 is lower than that of the T-72 series tank.

There are encouraging signs that Polish defence industry has begun the process of reform and consolidation. The transfer of NATO technology, combined with some high quality domestic designs, capable of competing in world markets, suggest the direction of change. By combining cooperation with Western firms, technology transfer, and competition in the world's weapons market, Polish defense industry can preserve its core capacity while it innovates in selected areas.

A good example of the latter is the 'Drawa-T' fire control system for the T-72 tank that the Poles have sold to India as part of a program to modernize 250 T-72 tanks in service with the Indian armed forces. The 'Drawa-T' contract is valued at $72 million. Clearly, Polish hardware can be competitive in some markets. In March 2002, Poland reached an agreement to supply its most modern PT-91 tank to Malaysia. The estimated value of the PT-91 contract is $250 million over the next ten years.[9]

Poland's Contribution to NATO

In March 1999 Poland, along with Hungary and the Czech Republic, was brought into NATO largely because of a political calculation. The country's potential military contribution was a secondary consideration at the time. Over the past three years Poland has performed very well politically, reforming its military institutions and acting as a loyal and dedicated member of NATO. The main problem area today is to ensure that Poland's military contribution to the alliance would be commensurate with the country's size and potential.

Poland proved to be a reliable ally when it was tested in the Balkan campaign immediately after accession, and subsequently contributed to Balkan peacekeeping operations. The Polish units and the Polish-Ukrainian battalion in Kosovo Force have performed well. Although Polish military contributions to the allied operations in the Balkans, and most recently, in Afghanistan, have been limited, the quality of the troops and their professionalism have earned the Poles high marks.

At the political level, Poland has demonstrated the strength of elite and public support for allied missions that can be considered exemplary. This high level of support for NATO and the country's participation in NATO operations is the highest among the three new entrants, as reflected by the polls conducted after the Balkan campaign.[10]

The military side of the equation presents a more complicated picture. The Polish armed forces lack in equipment and readiness. As NATO evolves, the alliance will rely less on forces that offer credible conventional defense, and more on forces suitable for NATO missions outside of allied territory. Poland, as a member of NATO, must not only be able to accept help from other nations, but also deliver its own contributions quickly and effectively, often to areas lying outside of NATO.

Like Hungary and the Czech Republic, Poland is currently maintaining 'two militaries': a small showcase force that is being made available for NATO operation and the largely legacy-based post-Soviet military establishment that contributes little and constitutes a drain on the limited national resources. In order to change this, the Polish armed forces may need to be downsized beyond the current targets; otherwise, the 2001–2006 program may unravel like its predecessors.

Additional savings from deeper personnel cuts would allow the country to move to a smaller, higher quality, more projectable and sustainable military force. The current target of a 150,000 strong army could perhaps be reduced further, possibly to 100,000 personnel. For example, additional reductions in the size of the land forces, projected for roughly 89,000 under the current program (a goal that amounts to a 70 per cent reduction of the land forces relative to 1989 where it stood at 310,000), could release resources for equipment and training. As stipulated in the program, Poland also needs to increase the proportion of its forces that are interoperable with NATO to at least one third of the total.

The target size of the Polish military directly affects the per capita spending in the armed forces. Assuming that no additional money will be coming from the budget, Poland can hope to double the per capita spending on the military only through further reduction in personnel. Likewise, without further reductions in the size of the armed forces, Poland will not be able to reach the stipulated 25–30 per cent share of the total expenditure on weapons and support systems.

Another persistent issue is the ratio of officers to NCOs. The Polish armed forces need to work to increase the number of NCOs, reduce the number of senior officers, and most importantly, rotate officers with experience in NATO structures into appointments where their expertise can best be utilized. Achieving the target of 30 per cent officers, 30 per cent warrant officers, and 40 per cent NCOs by 2006 is questionable without further personnel reductions.

Equipment modernization will remain the number one problem for the coming years. The torturous process of selecting a new multi-purpose fighter finally yielded a decision in December 2002. Still, according to the defence ministry, even if a smaller contract for 48 aircraft is signed at that time, the first deliveries could be expected in 2005, with the integration of the new Polish aircraft into NATO operations no sooner than 2008. Funding even for a reduced aircraft acquisition program remains in question given the country's worsening economic situation. In fact, considering the current debt repayment schedules, Poland is unlikely to have the money to pay for the new aircraft anytime before 2010. The contract, which is estimated at close to $4 billion, also requires at least a 100 per cent offset agreement mandated by law.[11]

It is unrealistic to expect that the Polish armed forces can replace their legacy systems with modern Western equipment any time soon. Still, a serious effort is needed to improve maintenance and readiness. The same applies to infrastructure. Both could be difficult to achieve, as the resources stipulated in the 2001–06 program for FYI 2002 could prove to be less than the plan had called for. The projected shortfall of 1.5 billion zlotys this year bodes ill for the future of the program, raising the specter that Poland will yet again revisit the issue of developing a viable plan for military modernization.

The situation is further complicated by the fact that, while building up forces for NATO missions, Poland needs to retain a modicum of territorial defense capability. The two goals put competing pressures on the scarce resources.[12]

Even if additional budgetary allocations for modernization are found, some deficiencies will simply take time to correct. Changes in personnel policy aimed at increasing the number of professional soldiers will take time to work themselves through the system. The same is true of the increase in requisite English language skills, which are still low, especially at the NCO level.

The 3 per cent of gross domestic product for defence, first promised during the Walesa presidency, was never realistic. In contrast, the current Polish military modernization program has set minimum targets both in terms of the overall outlays on defence and by offering a five-year commitment that makes planning possible. These goals should be implemented if the country's armed forces are to become a modern NATO military. Unfortunately, the defence ministry's ability to meet even those modest spending targets is today in doubt, as Poland faces rising unemployment and worsening economic conditions. Should the 2001–2006 program share the fate of its predecessors, this would relegate Poland to a second-tier status in the alliance for years to come.

NOTES

1. Briefing at the Land Forces Command, Warsaw, May 2001.
2. Author's interviews with Polish Ministry of Defense officials and General Staff officers, January–June 1995, Warsaw.
3. *The Armed Forces of the Republic of Poland* (Warsaw: Ministry of Defense, Jan. 1995).
4. Jeffrey Simon, *NATO Enlargement and Central Europe: A Study in Civil-Military Relations* (Fort McNair, MD: National Defense Univ. 1996) pp.26–27.
5. I refer to the pattern of transitional civil-military relations in post-communist Poland as the 'soldier-citizen' paradigm. See Andrew A. Michta, *The Soldier-Citizen: The Politics of the Polish Army after Communism* (NY: St Martin's Press 1997).
6. 'Gonimy sojusznikow', *Rzeczpospolita*, 31 Jan. 2001.
7. 'NATO's New Members Battle to Upgrade Their Military Punch', *The Financial Times*, 11 July 2001.
8. Zbigniew Lentowicz, 'Dwa skrzydla mysliwca', *Rzeczpospolita*, 12 Dec. 2001.
9. 'Malaysia to Buy Polish Tanks, Malaysian Premier Says', BBC Monitoring, 23 March 2002.
10. Based on polling conducted a year after NATO enlargement by the Center for Public Opinion Research in Warsaw (CBOS), the Institute for Public Opinion Research in Prague (IVVM), and the Center for Information Technology and Public Opinion Research in Budapest (TRKI).
11. Zbigniew Lentowicz, 'MON: mysliwiec niepolityczny', *Rzeczpospolita*, 1 March 2002.
12. Janusz Onyszkiewicz, 'Polskie wojsko i potrzeby paktu', *Rzeczpospolita*, 14 Feb. 2002.

From Security Consumer to Security Provider – Poland and Transatlantic Security in the Twenty-First Century

KERRY LONGHURST

As a member of the North Atlantic Treaty Organisation (NATO), but not yet of the European Union (EU), Poland is both an 'insider' and 'outsider' of the institutional framework that governs European security. This situation brings with it crucial dilemmas that Warsaw must manage in what is a highly dynamic and rapidly changing security environment. As the EU moves to consolidate its European Security and Defence Policy (ESDP) and NATO's engagement with the countries of Eastern Europe in the framework of the Membership Action Plan intensifies, the tenets of European security are being fundamentally modified and as this occurs new institutional synergies are created and new dynamics in regional security emerge. In this context, it is vital that, as an insider/outsider, Poland ensures that first and foremost its voice and interests are clearly articulated and fully acknowledged and second, that Warsaw understands the type of role its allies expect it to play in the coming years.

This article will consider Poland's role in Transatlantic and European security from the vantage point of the institutional perspectives of the EU and NATO. Inclusion of an institutional perspective in this study is important since Polish security policy has become heavily and irretrievably 'multilateralised' over the past few years. Even prior to Poland joining NATO in 1999 the prospect of membership provided the overarching impulse for the redirection and modernisation of the Polish armed forces. On route to creating its own security capability the European Union is also now acting as an 'agenda setter' for the evolution of Polish security policy in that it is shaping, if not determining national priorities and the pace of defence sector reforms.

In short, the 'NATO factor' and now the 'EU factor' provide the frameworks within which Warsaw is constructing its security policy, not least via the standards set by the Alliance's Defence Capabilities Initiative (DCI) and the EU's 'Headline Goals'.

The 'view from Brussels' provided here will identify and discuss some broad assessments of Poland's performance in the security sphere over the past few years, before highlighting some specific expectations and demands which are now placed upon Poland by the institutions. The principle message that this analysis seeks to communicate is that NATO and the EU expect Poland to take the necessary steps to shift from being a 'net consumer' of security, as it currently is, to take on the role of a 'net security producer'. This shift of role, it is argued, is essential if Poland's voice and interests are to be fully recognised by its allies.

Security Consumers and Security Producers

Notions of net security consumers and net security providers or producers are extremely useful and evocative concepts with which to consider Poland's emerging role within the Euro-Atlantic security complex. The idea is quite simple, it refers to the relative balance between what states 'gain' and what they 'give' within the context of a particular security complex or institution.

The problem is, though, how to decipher a consumer from a producer and is one totally distinct from the other? A rather crude way of determining which states are net-producers from those which are net-consumers would be to compare defence spending per gross domestic product and other material contributions made by individual states relative to their size.

Another method would be to classify states along the lines of whether they are 'passive' or 'active' in their security policies.

Both of these methods, it is argued here, are not sophisticated enough to take account of other important factors, such as geographical location, the export of know-how or specialist aptitudes, all of which determine the *ways* and means through which states' consume and produce security, which will also vary over time and contexts.

Hence there is a problem with the classification of consumers and providers of security, nevertheless it is a useful template with which to examine the transformation of Polish security policy.

Distinctions between net producers and net consumer of security were perhaps clearer to make during the Cold War. The Federal Republic of Germany of 1949–90 has been posited as the archetypal net-consumer of security during the Cold War. With a relatively low defence budget of its own and with a constitutional ban on the use of its own troops, Bonn consumed the security provided by the stationing of allied troops and nuclear weapons on its territory.[1]

The end of the Cold War threw the balance between net- providers and consumers of security into disarray. After 1989 it is far more problematic to ascertain which states are the producers of security and which are the consumers, since security as a commodity now has a far more amorphous quality. Having said this it is possible to outline the key attributes of security providers. In order to be providers or producers of security states must have a full range of military and non-military tools to carry out a variety of crisis management tasks.

In turn, in order to work, these attributes require steady and predictable national defence budgets grounded in a broad domestic consensus to ensure continuity of strategic priorities.

Tied to this, security producers need to be able to focus a greater proportion of their defence spending on research and development, to be able to have at hand modern and well-equipped readily deployable forces.

The overwhelming desire from Brussels is that Poland needs to take on the attributes of a modern security provider with all of the responsibility that this entails. This expectation largely correlates with the broad direction of change that Poland has already enacted, namely of beginning to modernise its armed forces and of making its defence spending more efficient. This point notwithstanding the emphasis placed by Brussels is that Poland's assumption of the role of security provider should take place at a swift pace and certainly sooner than the current round of Polish defence reforms suggest.

Evaluating Poland's Performance

When evaluating the strengths and weaknesses of Poland's membership in NATO since 1999 and its engagement with the development of ESDP, it is almost inevitable that commentators and policy makers make comparisons with the Czech Republic and Hungary. More often than not the view is taken that Poland is the far more significant partner and ally in East Central Europe and over the 1990s has developed in to a 'good institutional citizen' with a very 'together operation' and an effective and discernible voice. Much of this political capital was earned by Poland through its engagement in the Kosovo war, when Warsaw acted 'as an ally' and 'passed with flying colours' only shortly after joining the Alliance.[2]

Poland's broad and unconditional support for the US-led campaign against the Taliban in Afghanistan has further confirmed Warsaw's solid commitment to multilateralism. Soon after assuming his position the new Social Democrat (SLD) defence minister Jerzy Szmajdzinski stressed that Poland would not remain a 'passive' participant in the anti-terrorist coalition.[3]

Poland's credentials as the most dependable and pro-active ally among her neighbours in ECE were also evident when President Kwasniewski convened an Anti-Terrorism conference with leaders from Central, Eastern and South Eastern Europe on 6 November 2001. The event and details of the subsequent Action Plan demonstrated Poland's leadership qualities, commitment to the American-led campaign and to the tightening of regional security cooperation. Matching words with deeds started to become a reality at the end of November when, after a period of intense negotiations with the US, President Kwasniewski announced that Polish troops would be sent to Afghanistan beginning in early January 2002.

The events of 11 September 2001 also gave rise to a renewed impetus for Poland to act as 'conduit' for those countries in Eastern Europe aspiring to join Western institutions. Speaking in November President Kwasniewski argued that Poland's place in the post-11 September world order was to 'act as a leader to coax Eastern nations into the Western camp and to persuade the West to accept them'.[4]

There is overall a great deal of praise for the way in which Poland has adapted to the institutional frameworks of NATO membership, as well as the niche role Warsaw is carving in its Eastern policies, especially after 11 September. However, in part as a result of Poland's broad success, Warsaw's allies now have even greater expectations for a sustained high performance, which goes above and beyond the role expectations attached to the other NATO newcomers, the Czech Republic and Hungary.

Fulfilling Expectations – Becoming A Security Provider

With expectations high, the EU and NATO point to a range of specific issues and topics for Polish security policy to address. Importantly, these are not inflated expectations for a radical departure from current trends in Polish security policy, but rather entail a sustained commitment to those objectives already in motion, coupled with a more focused and timetabled programme of defence sector reforms.

Ensuring Poland's Voice in European Security and Defence Policy (ESDP)

The main forum for Poland to engage in ESDP matters is the 15+6 framework, which brings together EU member states with the six non-EU European NATO states. Thus far the 15+6 framework has been widely regarded as unsatisfactory in several ways. The 'six' have pointed to the rather vague and overly general nature of discussions and have called for a more detailed agenda for the meetings. On the other side the EU bemoans the often de-constructive manner in which the six have approached the forum and in particular the obsessive attitudes of some states towards the structure and framework of consultation.

As stated at the start of the article, one of the key tasks for Poland, as well as other non-EU NATO states is to ensure that its 'voice' is clearly articulated and fully recognised. This is particularly significant in the context of ESDP, with the crucial point being that it is the *way* in which Poland voices its interests in the development of ESDP and not the 'volume' of its voice, which will determine the response from Brussels. In essence, the main message coming from Brussels is that Poland must avoid becoming another Turkey. The effects of Turkey's intransigence over this matter invariably disabled the work of the 15+6 forum in the eyes of the EU and also served to breakup any sense of 'kinsmanship' built on common interests and concerns which had previously existed within the group of six non-EU, NATO states.

Although the Turkish position has subsided to an extent,[5] it is still imperative that Poland maintains a distance from the more obstructive actors in the 15+6 grouping, since the EU is clearly tiring from the lack of real constructive progress in the work of the group. Tied to this, it is important that Poland realises that the 15+6 forum is not the only opening for Poland to contribute to the shaping of ESDP and should not therefore be regarded as the sole route for Warsaw to pursue and to exercise its voice. By focusing on emerging processes and the opportunities they bring, rather than on structures, Poland will profit more from ESDP.

'Process not Structures'

Much has been done over the previous two years to help bridge the gap that persisted hitherto between the EU's declaratory security policy ambitions and its actual physical capabilities. Importantly for Poland many of these ongoing developments bring about new opportunities for Warsaw to engage with and to shape the nature of ESDP. A framework for decisionmaking in ESDP has been put in place in so far as the three interim committees for politico-military consultation were made permanent in early 2001.

The political and security committee (PSC) is the lynchpin body and will monitor international developments of relevance to the Common Foreign and Security Policy (CFSP). It will also aid the design of policy by drawing up opinions for the Council's consideration either in response to the latter's request or on its own initiative. The PSC will also monitor policies once implemented and will thus play a crucial role when the EU actually begins to deploy its own forces, exercising 'political control and strategic direction' of the EU's military response to crises. The PSC is also the leading body in discussions with the six non-EU NATO members as well as with NATO as a whole.

Alongside the PSC, the EU military committee (EUMC) and military staff (EUMS) were also made permanent at the beginning of 2001.

The drive of the Belgian Presidency (second half of 2001) was to produce a thorough stocktaking of its military assets, therefore it will become easier for Poland to engage with the development of the EU's security policies and specifically by being able to offer Polish contributions to the ESDP identified as areas of shortfall by the EU. Poland's capacity to engage with ESDP will also become more considerable with the EU and NATO's consolidated working relationship, in the form of a 'security agreement'. This overarching agreement will *inter alia* set out the procedures for the use of NATO assets by the EU.

All in all, the emerging processes creating ESDP that the EU has set up over the past 12 months appear more or less to satisfy any earlier concerns that Poland had regarding its status and role in this area.[6] Although proposals stop short of meeting Poland's desire to have a permanent Polish fixture within the Council, it is difficult to see how, as an EU outsider, Poland, as well as the other five, could be more involved in ESDP.

In truth it will only be when the first ESDP operation takes place that the real implications for Poland will become plain. And it will only be when the cooperative mechanisms between the EU and NATO are put to the test and the extent to which the committee of contributors can exact an influence is shown.

In the meantime, the coming months are crucial for Poland and for ESDP. During this time Poland has to overcome its concern with structures, especially the 15 + 6 forum, and start to get to grips with the nitty-gritty of the policy substance.

Poland as a Regional Stabiliser

Poland's particular added-value for Western institutions is already seen as deriving in a large part from the positive new synergies Warsaw has brought through enhancing both the EU's, but especially NATO's dialogue with Russia, together with the firming-up of the partnership with Ukraine. Indeed, it is widely regarded that Poland has already begun to take on the characteristics of security provider in that it has 'exported' security through its active commitment to the democratic reform processes of its eastern neighbours and by supporting the further enlargement of NATO and notional issue of a future EU enlargement to include Ukraine.

Unsurprisingly, the overwhelming desire emanating from Brussels is that Poland should continue to act as a force for stability in Eastern Europe. Poland's once disadvantageous geographical position bordering Kaliningrad and Ukraine at the outermost border of NATO and in the future the EU, is of great strategic importance and actually compels Warsaw to play a defining role in consolidating democratic transitions in this region, principally in the spheres of military reform, civil-military relations, the route to a future NATO enlargement and through the EU's Northern Dimension (ND).

Much of the added value Poland has brought to the Alliance draws from the experience Warsaw has of the countries to the East, especially through its membership in the Warsaw Pact until 1991. Language skills, cultural understanding and an appreciation of diplomatic styles that Poland acquired during this period have become assets for Poland, which Warsaw must capitalise upon. The view from Brussels of the new NATO members is that Poland alone has the statue and 'cognitive capacity' to work effectively with Eastern Europe and that this has already reaped huge benefits by enhancing the Alliance's relations with Russia and dialogue with Ukraine.[7]

Equally, it is widely regarded that since becoming a NATO member, Polish-Russian relations have become the healthiest they have ever been. Having said this, historical sensitivities and an atmosphere of mistrust prevails between Warsaw and Moscow and, as seen recently in discussions between Russia and NATO, Poland has not been as forthcoming as Brussels had hoped. Poland's initial reluctant attitude towards British Prime Minister Tony Blair's proposal for a strengthening of Russia's voice within NATO and request for 'clarification' is symptomatic of Warsaw's overall stance.[8]

Talking more specifically, much of the expectation placed upon Poland to be a security provider lies in the context of the second wave of NATO enlargement. This expectation from Brussels meshes neatly with Warsaw's desire to realise a swift enlargement, which is evident in the degree to which Poland is engaged in facilitating the Alliance's 'Membership Action Plan' (MAP). MAP represents a very different type of deal to that offered by the Alliance to Poland, Hungary and the Czech Republic in the 1990s, indeed it is explicitly stated that it is 'not' a direct route to NATO membership nor a 'checklist' to gain accession. Rather MAP, together with Partnership for Peace, is aimed at providing a framework for aspiring NATO members to guide them towards the types of requirements necessary to join the Alliance.

The essence of NATO's expectation is that through Poland's own experience of instigating defence reforms and joining the Alliance, Warsaw should now act as a positive role model for those countries to its East. However, it must be noted that the ability of Poland, Hungary and the Czech Republic to complete their own military reforms to fully reach NATO standards, is also necessary if NATO enlargement Part II is to happen. The lessons learned from the accession of Poland, Hungary and the Czech Republic into NATO will inevitably define the Alliance's collective position on the shape the second wave of enlargement should take. Consequently, ongoing obstacles and problems associated with Poland's aptitude to meet NATO standards may hinder the entire process and with it some central Polish interests.

Defence Sector Reforms

While both the EU and NATO recognise that Polish security policy has travelled huge distances over the past ten years and that the current reform programme goes beyond mere cosmetics and does contain some tough choices, the substance and pace of Warsaw's reforms suggest that Polish grand strategy remains guided by a 'defence' rather than a 'security' rationale. In short, Poland's rather 'old-fashioned' strategic stance and inappropriately structured armed forces means that in military terms Poland is not yet considered to be an asset.

The view emanating from NATO is that whereas Poland's 'accession' into the Alliance was completed in 1999, its more comprehensive 'integration' still proves elusive. There remains a great deal of work to be done if Warsaw expects to assume the role of first-rate and influential member of an enlarged Alliance.

Similarly, the EU anticipates a more concerted effort at defence reforms geared specifically to meet the requirements of the Headline Goals.

Although Warsaw is scheduled to have met the basic requirements set by the DCI and Headline Goals by 2006, the timeframe of the Polish reform programme is still regarded as being too slow.[9] Brussels requires that Poland not only moves to complete the reforms well before the current six-year time scale, but also that it goes above and beyond the scope. This is important since, as noted above, the amount of leeway open to Poland to instigate the necessary reforms and modernisation of its defence sector is rapidly diminishing, adding to the pressures for Warsaw to speed up the momentum. Consequently, by the time of the review of the enlargement process in 2002, Poland will be judged on an equal footing with older NATO members.

The reform impulse was revived in Poland in the wake of 11 September 2001 with Defence Minister Jerzy Szmajdinski outlining a plan to make the armed forces both more flexible for deployments as well as more adaptable to the market economy, with the bulk of military spending going towards rapid reaction forces.[10]

Twinned with this, other modernisation tasks were outlined as including the introduction of new command and communication systems and the acquisition of jet fighters. Szmajdinski's ambitions have, however, been tempered by a prohibitive budgetary situation which has already put a halt to the decision to acquire jet fighters.[11]

On the issue of finance, consternation is rife in Brussels at Warsaw's inability to increase its defence spending. Consistently declining levels of spending on defence since 1999, coupled with inefficiency of funds spent has put Warsaw under fire. Since joining the Alliance in 1999 Poland's overall defence expenditure has fallen from 2 per cent of gross domestic product to 1.8 per cent in 2001 with only nine per cent of the defence budget (2001) being allocated to equipment.[12]

This situation was recently exacerbated in December when the Sejm approved a financial package of savings, which are set to reduce defence spending by 2.1 billion zlotys.[13]

Conscription

Within the sphere of defence sector reforms concern is particularly acute surrounding the issue of conscription in Poland, which is viewed as a misplaced priority and a symptom of a lack of a thorough national debate on the merits and aptitude of the draft. Although there is no official NATO or EU policy on the future of conscription in Poland, there is an assumption in Brussels that Poland would begin the winding down of the practice in line with the general trend elsewhere in Europe. Expectations for change in Poland arose in the wake of the Czech Republic's programme of radical defence reforms outlined in summer 2001, which announced that conscription would be abolished by 2007.

Against this context of change the continuation of conscription in Poland and its seeming enhancement in the current reform process is somewhat bewildering to Brussels institutions.[14] Warsaw's belief that the maintenance of conscription will not hinder efforts at modernisation is not shared by Brussels, where it is understood that a commitment to the draft will hamper Poland's overall performance, by constituting a considerable drain on overall defence spending.

Although in his post-11 September plans for defence reorganisation Szmajdinski emphasised the need for the growing professionalisation of the armed forces, he stressed the continued vitality of conscription, given Poland's position on the 'edge of the NATO block'.[15] This steadfast commitment to keeping conscription conflicts head on with NATO and EU priorities and scenarios. Brussels thinking is that not only is an Article-5 type operation on NATO soil necessitating a large land-based force highly unlikely, but also that conscripts are ill suited for Petersburg-type tasks. The point made is that Poland's commitment to conscription is tied to an old fashioned conception of security policy based on territorial defence.

As mentioned above, although neither NATO nor the EU exacts a policy on conscription in Poland, there is a clear desire to see Warsaw switch to an all-volunteer-force (AVF). A Polish declaration to this end would enhance NATO's satisfaction with the Polish reform process and with it instil a sense of confidence in Warsaw's ability to deliver in the future.

Building Polish Strategic Culture

This final aspect is more fundamental and far-reaching in nature and will only emerge over time through a sustained national effort. The notion of strategic culture denotes more than traditional issues of civil military relations, entailing the manifold ways in which armed forces and the entire gamut of security institutions and processes relate to society. Both the EU and NATO impress upon all states in East Central Europe the need to keep up a sustained effort at forging a new strategic culture.

Clearly throughout the 1990s Poland began to shed its pre-1989 strategic culture, though this process is far from complete and a new entity has yet to fully transpire. That fact that democratic civil-military relations have been established, that parliamentary oversight is ensured and that women now serve within the armed forces are testimony to the extent to which change has been achieved.

However, it is apparent that a great deal of policy inertia limits the pace of further change and therefore strong elements of the former strategic culture remain in place and will do so unless military and defence sector reforms are approached in a more comprehensive fashion. Two particular issues stand out here as essential constituents for a new Polish strategic culture; the nurturing of a strategic community and the overhauling of the personnel system of the armed forces.

Forging an Effective Strategic Community

Although Poland has long since had in place all necessary components and institutions for democratic civil-military relations there remains a dearth of solid civilian know-how in defence matters, which both the EU and NATO see as debilitating for the effective functioning of Polish security policy and the modernisation of the military. The existence of a civilian strategic community is regarded as a 'frequently neglected', indeed misunderstood, aspect of democratic control and a 'common failing, with often disastrous results'.[16]

Poland's inability to construct a viable strategic community is not unique, and is common to all post communist states to varying degrees. The relatively rapid turnovers of governments have meant that among all former communist states there has not been an opportunity to nurture civilian expertise in foreign and defence ministries in security and defence matters. This, in turn, has led to a situation where a greater reliance has been placed upon advice from the military. As Christopher Donnelly writes, during the 1990s, a military establishment tended to close ranks to 'protect itself' when confronted with new ideas. Consequently funds intended for major reforms and rationalisation were often sucked in to merely sustaining the current system. Attempting to create the momentum for 'bottom-up' reform, senior officers were sent to the West for training and education. On their return, however, they were 'either dismissed, demoted or sent to serve in a dead-end post'.[17]

In this scenario, with the general failings of the bottom-up approach to reform the importance of the civilian strategic community and its role in promoting and sustaining change becomes paramount. The consequences of having only a small civilian strategic community are seen by Brussels as often ineffective decision-making, stymied communication between the Polish delegations in Brussels and Warsaw and the continuation of conscription and the lack of an adequate national debate about it's relevance.

Overhauling Poland's Personnel System

As mentioned above, the greater professionalisation of the Polish armed forces with more combat ready troops is a goal that both the EU and NATO want Warsaw to prioritise. Coupled with this, the effective internal organisation of the Polish military more in line with Western-style modals, is viewed as essential if Poland is to become a security provider.

This expectation from Brussels meshes with some policy objectives set out by Szmajdzinski in November 2001. At the heart of the objectives lies the need to make officer career paths more 'transparent', with any training gained within NATO providing as much credit as domestic operations. Twinned with this, the traditional officer schools and academies are destined to fold, though this will not be without sizeable obstruction from the military. In place of officer schools, officer candidates will come from civilian institutions, which will equip them with a range of skills transferable to life after the armed forces. Such reforms will ease the current crisis in the military education system, which has given rise to a surplus of young officers. Such ambitions are greeted in Brussels with approval, not least because they will help root out the blockages in the reform and modernisation processes caused by structural problems in the personnel system.

In contrast to the surplus of officers, the Polish armed forces have suffered from poor recruitment at the level of NCOs. From the vantage point of Brussels, what lies at the core of the problem here is the issue of the position of the armed forces in society and again conscription. Although the Polish armed forces have never suffered from the lack of prestige in society, either before or after 1989, the vocation of the professional soldier as a career choice for young men is generally not viewed as attractive, especially by more educated individuals. Already this poses a problem for the Polish military, especially in terms of morale among the lower ranks. What needs to be recognised is that conscription is not effectively serving the purpose of acting as a tool for recruitment. The reality is that since it is generally the lesser-educated young men who serve as conscripts, while their university-educated peers perform either civic service or delay their entry in to national service.[18]

Conclusion

The overall impression gleaned in this survey is that Warsaw is regarded as a good institutional citizen and has out-performed the other new NATO member states. Poland's broad successes and adaptability, especially to the political demands of NATO membership, have, however, had the effect of raising expectations and demands even higher. This is true to such an extent that Poland's ability to fully redirect its security policies is under increasingly close scrutiny and are regarded as a measure for the second round of NATO enlargement.

The message from Brussels is clear. Even with its insider-outsider status, in the emerging dynamics of European security Poland's position is of increasing importance and that the expectations for Warsaw to perform are extremely high.

Dealing with the range of issues detailed here will, however, necessitate the demarcation of priorities and entail some tough choices with broad social and economic implications. Amid this array of competing priorities, one issue stands out as requiring immediate attention; by signalling a willingness to abandon conscription several other issues can be worked out. As part of an overall reduction in the size of the armed forces, the winding down of conscription will enable Warsaw to spend more on equipping the military for the most likely types of future missions. Just as importantly, such a declaration will have a huge symbolic value, demonstrating to the EU and NATO that Poland is no longer tied to a territorial 'defence' rationale in its security policy.

In conclusion, there is in Brussels the expectation that Poland assume the role of security provider as soon as possible. This expectation correlates with the general direction of change being enacted in the Polish defence sector. However, while having the potential and desire to take up this role, confused priorities coupled with a sluggish pace of reform threaten to thwart Poland's ability to make the switch from net consumer of security to net provider in the twenty-first century.

NOTES

 1. Franz Josef Meiers 'Germany: The Reluctant Power', *Survival* 37/3 (Autumn 1995) pp.82–103.
 2. R.C.Hendrickson, 'NATO Expansion to the East: NATO's Visegrad Allies: The First Test in Kosovo', *Journal of Slavic Military Studies* 13/2 (June 2000) pp.25–38.
 3. 'Poland wants to take active part in antiterrorist coalition', *BBC Monitoring*, UK, 13 Nov. 2001. Ft.com; 'Defence Minister ready for Polish troops to Afghanistan request by US', *BBC Monitoring Services*, UK, 15 Nov. 2001, ft.com
 4. 'Poland's President Kwasniewski serves as a Conduit for East-West Diplomacy' *The Wall Street Journal* 20 Nov. 2001.
 5. See 'Rays of Light' *The Economist*, 15 Dec. 2001, p.33.
 6. Confidential interviews at NATO HQ and Council of the European Union, Brussels.
 7. Confidential interview at NATO HQ, Brussels, July 2001.
 8. Martin Walker, 'Russia's Big Step to NATO Worries Poles', *NATO Enlargement Daily Brief*, 26 Nov. 2001.
 9. Think piece written by Christopher Donnelly, NATO online library <www.NATO.int./docu/articles/2000/>.
10. 'Szmajdzinski's New Army Model', *Polish News Bulletin*, 19 Nov. 2001, Ft.com
11. See *Radio Free Europe Newsline*, 5/208, Part II (Nov. 2001).
12. There are only two NATO states which spend a lesser proportion of their defence spending on equipment; Belgium 5.4 per cent and Portugal 6.3 per cent (2001 figures).
13. Polish Lower House Passes Budget Savings Plan for 2002, *BBC Monitoring Service*, UK, 23 Dec. 2001.
14. Confidential interview at NATO HQ, European Council, Brussels, July 2001.
15. See note 10.
16. Donnelly (note 9).
17. Ibid.
18. See 'Europe's Sulky Conscripts', *The Economist*, 18 Aug. 2001, p.47.

Poland: America's New Model Ally

DAVID H. DUNN

In the aftermath of the terrorist attacks on America on 11 September 2001 the US has found itself in need of more allies than ever. In its efforts to build an international coalition Washington has decided to overlook substantial differences with many nations in its fight against terrorism. Thus while the diplomatic language used may speak of 'new allies' and 'renewed friendships' such talk does not disguise the fact that alliances come in many forms and serve many different purposes. Poland's new strategic relationship with the US, symbolised by its accession to NATO in March 1999, is a case in point. While US-Polish relations have remained singularly inconspicuous in the war against terrorism, Washington nevertheless continues to see Warsaw as an important new ally. For Washington, Poland is not only the regional leader in East Central Europe, it is also the model US ally in its policy of NATO expansion. In the wake of 11 September this policy, and thus US relations with Poland, are viewed with even greater importance. In the 'war on terrorism' that Bush has declared, any doubts about the continued validity of NATO have been completely dispelled in the American view.

The importance of Warsaw to the US was demonstrated by its choice to host a regional anti-terrorism conference in November 2001 in which President Bush participated by video link. Bush also chose Warsaw as the venue for his only major speech on his first visit to Europe in June 2001. These decisions were not coincidental. On both occasions Bush was recognising the fact that Poland has come furthest and fastest of all the former communist states. For his June speech Bush was not only choosing an enthusiastically pro-American audience. By using Warsaw to set out his administration's vision towards Europe the new administration was symbolising how America views Poland within Europe and NATO. Precisely how Washington sees Poland as a new NATO ally, and why, and how successful Poland has been in adapting to this role, is the subject of this contribution.

For Washington, Poland's successful transition to a democratic, free market capitalist state and enthusiastic NATO ally is a vindication not just of America's post-Cold War foreign policy. It is a vindication of containment as a whole, with Poland the gleaming prize of cold war victory. As Bush set out in his Warsaw press conference, America regards Poland 'as an example of what's possible' for former communist states.[1] Poland's emulation of what Washington sees as the American model is the template for all the new democracies of Europe. Not only does Poland's example justify the export of the American model; Warsaw's support for America strengthens the means to that foreign policy end. As Bush announced in Warsaw, with the US and Poland working in concert 'The question is no longer what others can do for Poland, but what America and Poland and all of Europe can do for the rest of the world.'[2]

Poland's political and economic transformation from communism has been remarkable, and an important aspect of that success has been the way in which it has established itself as a close and trusted ally of the United States. Within 12 years Poland has gone from being a member of a hostile military alliance – the Warsaw Pact - to being regarded within the Washington policy community as a more trusted and valued ally than many long standing NATO members. As the *Washington Post* has noted, Poland is 'more supportive of the United States diplomatically than Germany or France'.[3]

While this new relationship reflects a shared commonality of interest, it is also the product of an explicit policy by both parties to make this relationship work. As a new member of an old alliance Poland has also been able to benefit from NATO's established position without having had the trauma which so often characterised NATO's development. Thus in its relationship with Washington, Poland is unencumbered by any of the political baggage which has characterised transatlantic relations for many of the other allies.[4]

Its absence of experience of close dealings with Washington during the nuclear crises of the 1980s or the Balkan debacles of the 1990s colours its view of American diplomacy. As such Polish-American relations might well be characterised as still being in the honeymoon period. How this relationship will develop will be important not only for the bilateral relationship itself but also for America's relationship with Europe both inside and outside NATO.

Poland's efforts to establish close relations with Washington over the last decade or so have largely meant dealing with the democratic Clinton administration. With the White House now occupied by a new Republican administration with its own approach to international politics, it is a useful point at which to take stock of American-Polish security relations. Accordingly, this essay analyses how successful Poland has been at establishing itself as a valuable ally of the United States and on what basis that relationship is founded. How solid this relationship will remain in the face of possible policy differences is also analysed.

In order to do this the essay first analyses the background of the relationship. It then analyses what 'added value' Poland brings to NATO from the perspectives of the American policy community. It goes on to look at the issues of Poland's *Ostpolitik*; NATO's Article 5; NATO Enlargement; Ballistic Missile Defence; European Security and Defence Policy (ESDP), and Polish Defence Policy within NATO. How these issues contribute to making Poland America's new model ally will then be assessed.

Background

While Poland is one of America's newest NATO allies it is regarded by Washington as an old friend. Indeed, while the United States has several special relationships, such as those with the UK, and Israel, it is fair to say that America's relationship with the Republic of Poland qualifies for this status. Like America's other special relationships, the ties that bind are a mixture of historical, cultural and strategic bonds. Poland's historical ties go back to the late eighteenth century when many Poles fled their partitioned homeland to fight under George Washington in the American War of Independence. These ties were strengthened when President Woodrow Wilson championed Polish independence at the end of World War I.[5] They were furthered still during World War II when Poland's valiant resistance to the Germans won it considerable favour among the American public.

During the Cold War the radio broadcasts of the Voice of America and Radio Free Europe were also seen by many Poles as evidence that America had not forgotten their plight or abandoned hope for their future. The events of the 1980s were to further renew these ties. President Reagan's anti-Soviet stance and his rhetorical support for the Solidarity movement were warmly welcomed in Poland.[6] Similarly, the courage of the Free Trade Union Movement and the catalytic role that it played in the unravelling of the Soviet empire and state were greatly applauded in Washington.

The community of 10 million Americans who claim Polish descent is another source of that special relationship.[7] Chicago is reported to have the second largest 'Polish' population outside Warsaw. The concentration of that community in certain key states in the Northeast, and the political activism of its members in advancing Polish interests are a further factor in this relationship. Pressure from this constituency was an important factor in Poland's admission to NATO by the Clinton administration.[8] These historical ties and cultural connections help explain why opinion polls continually show that Americans are the Poles' favourite foreigners.[9] They also partly explain why Poland is such a loyal and valued ally of the United States.

The other part of that explanation, however, is a strategic calculation. Poland is concerned to safeguard its newly established autonomy against any possible future threats and has concluded that a close alliance with the United States within the Atlantic community and elsewhere is the best means to that end. As a June 2001 editorial in the Polish newspaper *Rzeczpospolita* explained, 'Poland has a tragic historic experience behind it, and it needs to have an ally on which it can depend.'[10]

For its part the US recognises the importance of a trusted and loyal ally both in its strategically vital position in Central Europe and in the international community more broadly. Poland's support for the US at the United Nations (UN) and in other international organisations is consistently favourable. Even on such controversial policies such as sanctions against Libya and the continuous bombing of Iraq, Poland's support is constant and uncritical. Warsaw's support for the US in its war on terrorism has been unequivocal. Unlike many European nations, Poland does not consider a UN mandate a necessary precondition for international military action.

For America, Poland's willingness to take an independent, robust and strategic approach to international politics, is one which is refreshing and very welcome. This commonality of worldview is one reason why Washington has entrusted the Polish Embassy in Baghdad to look after US diplomatic interests in Iraq. This example, if one were needed, illustrates the degree to which Poland has rapidly established itself as a trusted and important ally of the US.

Having looked at the 'why' of Polish-American relations it is now necessary to evaluate the 'how'. That is to say how Poland has contributed to its bilateral relationship with the US in order to make itself a valuable ally to Washington. Accordingly, the next section will look at Poland's added value to the US.

America's New Ally: Poland's 'Added Value'

While Poland enjoyed a warm relationship with the US during the Clinton years, its relationship with the Bush administration has been even more cordial. The tendency of the Bush administration to define its

foreign policy priorities largely in terms of America's self-interest inclines
it to be more openly supportive of the loyalty which Poland has displayed
towards Washington. This is especially evident since 11 September. The
Bush administration's focus on strategic calculations reinforces the vital
role that Poland continues to play in the process of transforming the
security environment of central Europe. The admission to NATO of a
stable, democratic Poland with the fastest growing economy in Europe has
extended the zone of peace and stability in Europe and the geographic
space of the alliance.

The significance of Poland's admission to the alliance, however, is
greater still, as Andrew Michta explains, 'Poland's membership of NATO
has the potential to dramatically change the regional equation and,
ultimately, to do away with a fundamental historical tenet of European
geopolitics: German-Russian competition for regional domination.'[11]

Certainly, the fact of Poland's membership has now made it possible
for Poland to engage Russia diplomatically without fear of renewed
Russian domination, and as a result has provided the opportunity for
Warsaw to play a role as a bridge between NATO and Russia. Given the
importance of NATO, being able to engage Russia successfully for all
European security matters, this may well prove to be Poland's most
valuable political contribution to the alliance. This is certainly a view
expressed in Washington.[12]

Poland's value to the United States, however, goes beyond the
successful way in which it has reconciled its traditional security dilemmas
in central Europe. Indeed, in every respect Poland has been explicit in its
efforts to make itself a self evidently good ally to Washington and by
extension to NATO. As Grudzinski has explained, 'Poland has tried to
utilise in the best way possible every opportunity to get closer to the
alliance, to prove it could contribute to the strengthening of NATO's
potential...to convince the alliance that we will be a provider, and not just
a consumer, of stability and security both now and in the future.'[13]

Poland's willingness to make its large military training facilities
available to the alliance was an early and obvious manifestation of this
commitment. This gesture was widely appreciated in Washington at a time
when other allies were facing tighter environmental and political
constraints on the availability of their training areas.[14]

Poland also pledged 300 troops to the US led 'war on terrorism' in
Afghanistan, a total that included special forces, chemical and biological
warfare experts and sappers.[15] Although these numbers represent more of
a symbolic contribution than a militarily significant one their political
importance should not be underestimated. In the wake of the invocation

of NATO's Article 5 security guarantee the willingness of American's allies to contribute to the collective defence has not gone unnoticed in Washington.

Perhaps the most tangible way in which Poland sought to demonstrate its contribution before the events of 11 September 2001 was in its deployment of peacekeeping forces to the Balkans. Not only has Warsaw deployed forces to Bosnia as part of the Implementation and Stability Forces, and contributed to the UN Preventive Deployment Force in Macedonia, it has also sent peacekeepers to Kosovo at every stage of the operation there. Poland's willingness to supply monitors for the potentially hazardous Organization for Security and Cooperation in Europe (OSCE) operation in Kosovo which preceded the 1999 NATO bombing campaign, was a commitment calculated to demonstrate Warsaw's reliability as an ally. This point was reinforced by the much more equivocal response of the other new allies, especially during the air campaign. Poland's willingness to deploy forces in Kosovo is even more remarkable given that the deployment required a change to the country's constitution and considerable technical difficulties in actually transporting the troops to the region by train.

Despite these difficulties Poland was also able to reinforce its contingent in Kosovo in 2000 with a further battalion in response to calls for more forces from the UN Secretary-General. The role played by these forces in Mitrovica was particularly appreciated by the United States whose own forces there were not always fully in command of the situation.[16] Presently Poland deploys 1,000 peacekeepers out of a total of 40,000 in Kosovo. Furthermore President Kwasniewski has signalled his willingness to deploy a larger Kosovo Force (KFOR) peacekeeping contingent if necessary.[17]

Such deployments not only demonstrate Warsaw's commitment to being good allies, but they also provide valuable training for Polish forces in NATO procedures, operational planning and in multilateral operations conducted in English. Participation in Operation 'Allied Force' also increased support for NATO and its mission within Poland.[18]

The procurement of two NATO compatible frigates from the United States is also intended to give Poland a capability to participate in naval peacekeeping operations and to be tasked to the Standing Naval Force Atlantic.[19] The latter commitment is an indication of Poland's view of its security interests as truly international. Its plans to procure six new German-designed frigates by 2004 to be built in Gdynia, is further evidence that Poland's naval role is seen as greater than the defence of the Baltic Sea.[20]

Further, Poland maintains a peacekeeping training facility dedicated to the creation of a cadre of troops versed in these skills, something that not all allies can boast.[21]

This commitment to peacekeeping together with Poland's supportive response to Operation 'Allied Force' in 1999, and Operation 'Enduring Freedom' in 2001, are seen in Washington as a vindication of American leadership in pushing the expansion of the alliance. They also serve to identify Poland as an ally who could be relied upon and, where militarily possible, as a potential future contributor to coalitions of the willing in Europe and elsewhere. At a time when America considers itself to be at war and is actively debating wider military action than that initially pursued against Afghanistan, Poland's support, politically and militarily, is appreciated in Washington.

Although not widely reported, Poland's intelligence services have proved a useful source of important human intelligence to the United States. Warsaw proved particularly helpful to the US and NATO during the Kosovo campaign. The penetration of the former Yugoslavia by Polish intelligence meant that NATO had an extremely good source of human intelligence assets in Serbia and Kosovo which were very useful in target identification and other roles.[22] Poland's willingness to share the products of its intelligence service with the US was a policy that greatly endeared Warsaw to Washington throughout the 1990s. In the first half of the 1990s Polish intelligence assets in Iraq and Iran were also most valuable to the US, making up for Washington's deficiencies in human assets in these countries.

Given Poland's well-established intelligence activities in the Middle East, it is also likely that Warsaw has been of assistance to Washington in its recent counter-terrorism activities. This was certainly an issue in the recent debate over efforts to bring the Polish security services under democratic control. The chiefs of both the internal and the external security services resigned in protest that the reorganisations would limit Poland's ability to help Washington to combat terrorism.[23] These reforms, however, were instigated as part of an effort to make the security services operate along Western principles.

In important ways then Poland has been instrumental in becoming a security contributor in its relationship with the United States. In these areas identified, Poland has been able to act in a way that has not been to the detriment of its own interests while being of assistance to its new ally. In the next section the major policy issues of the transatlantic agenda will be analysed to ascertain whether any conflicts of interests exist between Polish and American security relations.

Poland's *Ostpolitik*

Poland's *Ostpolitik* has been a central feature of its foreign policy since independence and it is an international role that it sees as of even greater importance post-11 September. Bringing the Eastern nations closer to the Western camp is a role that President Kwasniewski sees as ideally suited to Poland.[24] His visit to Moscow in October 2001 and his invitation to President Putin to visit Warsaw in January 2002 are the most visible evidence of his efforts to further establish this role.

Certainly, since independence for Warsaw in 1989 Poland's *Ostpolitik* has been of particular value to the United States as a new regional ally. This has been the case for two distinct and important roles. First as a model for aspiring NATO applicants, and second, as a reassurance to those states concerned about the strategic and political implication of the enlargement process. In the first role, Poland, along with Hungary and the Czech Republic, has been a model for all the states of Central and Eastern Europe of how to successfully 'return to Europe' through both its membership of NATO and its accession process with the EU. The special obligations that Poland was under as one of the first new members of NATO were acutely felt in Warsaw.

Here again, however, Polish and American security interests were in common. Both countries favoured the further enlargement of the alliance and both realised that US domestic support would only be forthcoming for such a policy if the first expansion was seen as a conspicuous success. Unless the new allies met their NATO responsibilities as fully as possible it would be extremely difficult for the process of further enlargement to proceed. Poland's role as the largest and most wealthy new ally was especially symbolic in this regard. As a result the successful way that it has managed the transition to alliance membership and the extent to which it has achieved the goals set for full NATO participation, are particularly well received in Washington. The US now regards Poland as the regional leader of Eastern Europe and as such it sees its transition from student to teacher in the NATO accession role as crucial.

Of equal importance for the US is the way in which Poland has managed its relations with the states of the former Soviet Union. By publicly embracing the NATO rationale for enlargement – expanding the zone of peace and stability eastward – Poland avoided any further deepening of Russia's antagonism which might have resulted from a more self-interested security oriented justification.

Similarly, the major reforms of the Polish armed forces have further reassured to its neighbours of Warsaw's intentions in joining NATO.

Poland's Ukraine policy has also contributed to regional security and is especially well regarded in Washington. America rightly regards Ukraine as a Polish speciality and is always willing to listen to and accommodate the views of the Polish Foreign Ministry on this subject. Polish–Ukrainian relations had the potential to be problematical but the way that Poland in particular has handled them has ensured both good bilateral relations and that Ukraine has stayed on a western orientation. Good relations exist at every level both officially and unofficially. Polish non-governmental organisation involvement in the Ukraine for example is more substantial and important than the role of the EU in promoting development. The Polish Embassy in Kiev until recently also represented NATO to the Ukraine, a fact that illustrated America's trust of Poland's management of this relationship.

Similarly, Polish diplomacy in Washington has also been effective in ensuring that State Department assessments of Ukraine for the Senate have not stood in the way of valuable loans for Kiev.[25] The creation in 1999 of the Polish American Ukraine Cooperation Initiative, a tri-governmental venture to use Polish expertise to direct American money towards Ukrainian need, is a further example of the crucial role which Poland plays towards Ukraine and the positive way in which this is viewed in Washington.

While Poland's relations with Russia inevitably suffered as a result of its accession to NATO in 1999, the fact of this new reality may actually prove the making of a more stable and secure bilateral relationship between Warsaw and Moscow. As Michta argues, 'So long as Poland remained outside the Western security system, relations between Warsaw and Moscow had focused predominantly on the settling of accounts from the past.'[26] With Poland's new sense of security following NATO accession, the agenda has moved on and relations have been conducted on a new foundation. Russia has accepted Poland's membership of NATO and a new, positive bilateral relationship now exists. Poland's new confidence in its dealings with Moscow also follows on from NATO membership. That NATO's first round of enlargement did not damage Russia's security was seen in Warsaw and Washington as a vindication of the policy. And that the process proceeded despite Moscow's objections was seen in Poland as evidence of the new realities of European security.

The accession of President Putin in Russia and his support for America's 'war on terrorism' post-11 September 2001 have also affected Poland's *Ostpolitik*. The closer ties between NATO and Russia have created a new climate of cooperation that has also affected Polish-Russian relations. There has been a marked increase in the amount of high-level bilateral diplomacy between Warsaw and Moscow which reflects the fact that past differences are being set aside in the new spirit of post-11 September 2001 cooperation.

The cooperative stance that President Putin has adopted towards the US since the terrorist attacks has also markedly changed the context of this aspect of Polish diplomacy. By providing Washington high level intelligence on Afghanistan, facilitating American diplomatic efforts in Central Asia and elsewhere and generally showing a less obstructive attitude towards missile defence and NATO expansion, Russia has undergone a major foreign policy shift.

One of the consequences of this move is that NATO and Poland's *Ostpolitik* has assumed a greater importance. That Poland has responded positively and cooperatively to these new developments from Russia, despite its own reservations about Putin's motivations, has further endeared Warsaw to Washington.

NATO's Article 5 Security Guarantee

For many, the invocation of NATO's Article 5 security guarantee in the wake of the terrorist attacks on America was indicative of the alliance's new role and relevance in the twenty-first century. For Poland, however, despite its improved relations with Russia, there is still a strong attachment to this provision of the Washington Treaty in its original twentieth century context. This residual concern with NATO's Article 5 security guarantee and with the security concern which that represents, is a cause of some irritation in some quarters in Washington.

There is, however, a range of opinion on this question. On the one hand Brzezinski argues that Poland's concerns are legitimate in the face of potential scenarios where Poland might need to be able to resist hostilities long enough to trigger a NATO response.[27] Others are understanding but more critical. Given its strategic position and history, it is argued, Poland can be forgiven for thinking as if it is the 'new Germany' within NATO, out on the edge, if not the front line of the alliance. The majority of opinion, however, sees little justification for thinking in this way. This view is even more strongly expressed in the wake of Russia's rapprochement with Washington following the terrorist attacks on America.

One former Clinton National Security Council (NSC) member commented that Poland's fixation on territorial defence was misplaced and that Warsaw needed to move on 'because there is Article 5, they could not stop them even if they came, and they are not coming'.[28] This slightly more detailed comment from another NSC member, this time from the

Bush administration, provides a fuller picture of the prevailing American view.

> We are the last ones to say that they should not think about territorial defence, after all they are in a tough neighbourhood, just look at their borders. That said, though, an armoured attack across their borders is not a likely prospect. There are no armoured divisions sitting across the borders ready to invade in the way there was for Germany during the Cold War. They are not the 'new Germany' in that sense. But we will not be saying that they should not have tank battalions. But they need to learn to take on board fully the mentality that goes with alliance membership. Their reaction to the news story about Russian deployment of nuclear weapons in Kaliningrad was symptomatic of an approach that suggested that they faced this issue on their own. They do not. They are a member of NATO, of 19 members. And they need to see things in an alliance context. Part of that means starting to think more about 21st century threats.[29]

This quotation provides a good summation of America's view towards Poland's security concerns. While they would like them to be less concerned about territorial defence and more concerned about their ability to build forces for power projection or peacekeeping, Washington understands Poland's thinking. And provided that provision for territorial defence is not provided at the expense of other roles and commitments then Washington will not be overly critical of this aspect of Polish policy.

In the longer term, however, Poland's ability to contribute its forces to roles relevant to the new threat environment may colour Washington's perceptions of Warsaw's security priorities. The fact that Poland could only initially offer 80 special forces soldiers to the coalition effort in Afghanistan and then not until January 2002 after they had had English language training, is an indication of how much Poland's armed forces are still configured to fight primarily twentieth century threats.

NATO Enlargement

Like the Article 5 issue, opinion in Washington on Poland's role in the NATO enlargement debate is split. For those who oppose further expansion Poland's support for this process is unwelcome.[30]

At the other extreme too there is disappointment. For the most enthusiastic proponents of further and wider enlargement there is a degree of frustration that the Poles have not been leading the debate in the US by an early and energetic activism. This criticism, which is most prevalent within Congress, is attributed to Poland's timidity in not wanting to overly upset any section of American elite opinion.[31]

It is, however, an opinion that reflects the high expectations that some participants in the debate have of Poland. Indeed there is a common expectation in Washington that Poland will play the role of the locomotive for enlargement. While more sober assessments realise that Poland's enthusiasm for the process can never be the same as when it represented its own security interests, there is nevertheless an expectation that Poland is well placed to lobby for the inclusion of new NATO members. As the new model ally, Poland's economic and political success and its unequivocal support for the United States within NATO makes Warsaw the exemplary model for further enlargement within Washington. That membership of the alliance has made Poland less 'frantic' about its security than it once was is cited as a positive benefit of membership for both Poland and Russia.

Furthermore, as an equal NATO member making their own case for enlargement, Poland's arguments are mutually supportive of the establishment view in Washington. That Poland does not talk about its own security but espouses the argument that the US uses, that enlargement is about spreading peace and stability eastwards, is recognised by many as a shrewd approach.

That further enlargement is likely to occur in 2002 to include at least Slovenia, Slovakia, the Baltic Republics and possibly others is widely, if not universally, accepted in Washington. Among supporters of a wider enlargement in Washington there is also the hope that Poland's considerable lobbying skills can be set to work to persuade fellow members to accept a wider membership.

As a consequence of the first round of expansion in 1999 it is widely believed that the path to further enlargement has been greatly eased, even though the first round was much less controversial than the second. Of the three arguments against enlargement during the first round, Poland's membership in particular has reduced their salience for 2002.

The first was cost. For the first round there were lots of studies then that suggested that the transition costs would be huge and that this would be a strain on the alliance.[32] These costs did not materialise partly because the pace of conversion has been much slower than some envisaged. This is in part due to a more relaxed attitude to threat perception, which is in itself a benefit of NATO membership. As a result of this cost is unlikely to be much of an issue in this next round.

The second argument concerns military effectiveness and is the main concern of the US armed forces and the Pentagon. Last time this argument was concerned about the effect of enlargement on the military capabilities and integrity of the alliance, the watering down of the world's finest military alliance.[33]

Because of the institution of the Membership Action Plan (MAP) process, however, the mechanisms now exist for questions of this nature to be analysed. There are planned to be two further MAP reviews before the 2002 summit. This process creates its own problems though as it also provides the opportunity for states to argue their case on this criterion alone. Thus while the Baltic republics are doing well on the MAP criteria it would be politically difficult to admit states that have done less well on these criteria while omitting Latvia, Lithuania, and Estonia.[34]

It will be hard to keep out those who are more qualified, which is another argument to include all the Baltic States.[35] That fact that Poland is more concerned than most about the military effectiveness of its allies and neighbours and yet is enthusiastic to support a wider enlargement is a powerful argument in the debate.

The third concern is what this means for Russia. There was a lot of concern on this account last time around from the *New York Times*, and various academic defence analysts. Enlargement was seen as needlessly provoking Russia and preventing its reintegration with Europe. The fact that Russia is even more engaged with the West than it was before 1999 will weaken this argument this time around as will the less hostile approach of Moscow towards enlargement altogether.

Poland's improved relationship with Moscow is also presented as evidence that better relations between Russia and its former satellites may actually follow enlargement. That this process will require delicate handling with the Russians is not in question. It is a process however, that may also provide Poland with a further opportunity to prove to Washington its value as a new ally.

Despite the concerns expressed about the consequences of NATO enlargement within the US debate, the decision that the Bush administration takes in recommending who should be admitted and when, will be heavily influenced by political factors. First among these is the way that the alliance is perceived in relation to America's 'war on terrorism'. For the US the fact that it has new international enemies and that its traditional allies have offered such trenchant support for Washington, has increased support for NATO and its further expansion.[36]

A second factor, though now less important than it once was, will be the desire for a foreign policy success demonstrating American commitment to Europe following strain within the Atlantic community over Kyoto, ballistic missile defence and the continued US commitment to the Balkans. A second round of enlargement would seem an attractive option to the new administration as agreement on this subject seems more attainable than in any other policy area.

The Senate too seems predisposed to support such a policy initiative and is in part inclined to do so as a result of the way in which Poland has behaved as a new ally.[37] Not only is Poland's conduct viewed as a vindication of the first round, its role in coaching the new applicants and in assuaging the concerns of those left out is seen as reassuring by Congress. In this respect Poland is an active participant in the process of enlargement well beyond its formal role as a new member. As such it continues, and will continue to be, a valuable ally to the US and to NATO as a whole in this entire process.

Ballistic Missile Defence

For Poland, unlike other US allies, the issue of ballistic missile defence does not represent a serious bone on contention between Washington and Warsaw. Indeed Poland has been more forthcoming than most European allies in its support for this initiative.[38] That is not to say, however, that Poland has not voiced its quiet concerns about the potential damage that this issue could do to alliance unity. Warsaw is realistic enough to appreciate, however, that outright opposition to this policy would be to fruitlessly risk the valuable relationship that it has built up with Washington. Poland also realises that the Bush administration remains firmly committed to the deployment of ballistic missile defence, even more so after 11 September, and will not be moved on this issue by allied concerns.

Although Bush's position represents a big change in US policy from the Clinton administration which, while paying lip service to the idea, was neither serious nor supportive of deployment, there is now near consensus within the Washington policy community that some sort of missile defence deployment is inevitable. Poland's recognition of this colours how it approaches this debate. Accepting that deployment will happen focuses attention on managing how to minimise the damage caused to the alliance by this process. It is here that Polish and American interests find common ground.

Once again, but for different reasons, Poland is in the position of being a supportive ally of America by pursuing its own security interests. In practice, however, Washington does not expect Poland to play an active role in this debate within Europe. Poland's ability to influence Europe in a positive way is recognised as limited and potentially counter productive.

So long as the Poles are not openly critical of the scheme Washington expects them to play a low profile role in the debate.[39]

European Security and Defence Policy (ESDP)

Rather like the issue of ballistic missile defences, the issue of the EU's plans for a military dimension to its Common Foreign and Security Policy has created common concerns and positions between the United States and Poland.

While the US has expressed concerns over the potential risks of duplication of effort and structures, discrimination against non-EU NATO members and disengagement between the two halves of the Atlantic, Poland's concerns have echoed those of Washington from a different corner of the alliance. Indeed Poland's concerns give substance to Washington's anxieties. For Warsaw the main concern is the creation of institutional ambiguity as to who would be responsible for a crisis in the Baltics, Kaliningrad, or over Belarus or Ukraine. In such circumstances, Poland fears, misunderstandings may result and decisions may be prolonged or postponed to the detriment of Polish security.

Similarly, as a non-EU member of NATO, Poland objects to discrimination against the six nations in its position who are excluded from EU decision making on matters of European security. Poland is also concerned that the rhetoric of ESDP without the economic commitment to built military capability might run the risk of alienating the United States without offering anything of substance in its place. As such, for its own security interests, the Polish position on ESDP is one of conditional acceptance only. As then Defence Minister Bronislaw Komorowski explained, Poland's security policy priorities are that, 'We want to maintain ties with the USA and its involvement in Europe. At the same time we support development of the European security and defence system. We want these activities to be harmonious.'[40]

Like the Bush administration, however, the Polish government realises that there is a certain inevitability over some form of ESDP and as such the most important approach to this policy initiative is one which seeks to manage its impact on the alliance rather than to fight it on principle. The position of the Bush administration is that it is supportive of ESDP if it is done right. If this initiative is successful it could help provide additional resources for the alliance and provide coordinated planning among EU states. The administration also wants it to succeed because its failure could be extremely problematic for NATO. As such it is keen to support every effort to ensure the positive development of this policy. In this it views Poland's role as mutually supportive and possibly decisive.

For some analysts Poland is seen as a crucial player in shaping the form that ESDP will take in practice. For these commentators, once Poland gains membership of the EU, its role in tempering the French vision of an autonomous defence identity for Europe is seen as pivotal to the continued engagement of the US in NATO in its present form. As such Poland's long term value to the US as an ally who shares Washington's concerns and perspectives on ESDP, is likely to remain important.

Polish Defence Policy

How useful an ally Poland can be within NATO and to the US more generally is in part dependent on Warsaw's successful implementation of military reform. Poland, along with the other two new NATO members certainly has serious obstacles to overcome as part of this process. As Jeffrey Simon explains, all three 'share the common experience and burden of the Warsaw Pact: inherited armed forces too big and too heavy for contemporary warfare, decaying Soviet military technology, an overabundance of infrastructure'.[41]

Even recognising these difficulties, however, the pace and manner of Poland's defence reforms has been subject to criticisms within the US. These criticisms range from the general to the specific. Generally, there is frustration at the slow pace of reform. It is noted that force goals adopted five years ago remain unimplemented largely due to a lack of political will and those reforms that have been done have tended to prioritise 'show-piece' units at the expense of the Main Defence Forces and Territorial Forces.[42] The criticism has also been made that the process of political and economic reform in Poland generally has been more successful in the competition for resources, political will and popular support than defence reform.

A related concern is that the relatively healthy state of the Polish economy draws away skilled personnel from the professional forces. Thus as the Polish armed forces are being reduced in size to a force of 150,000 by 2003, in the words of Robert Lipka, the Deputy Defence Minister, 'Unfortunately, the wrong people are leaving.'[43] Poor pay and conditions contribute to the problem of retention of the non-conscript element of the armed forces. As Jeffrey Simon explains, 'In the Polish Air Force, pilots have been departing in droves…[since] a pilot with 15 years experience earns roughly 3000 zlotys per month, while he can command 8000 zlotys on the open economy.'[44]

And yet efforts to improve conditions within the armed forces have also been met with complaints, reportedly from within NATO, that

'Poland's relatively high defence budget...is largely being wasted on military pensions and wages.'[45] Clearly, the balance between military efficiency and defence reform is not an easy one for Poland to resolve.

More strategic criticisms can also be found, however. For one critic 'The greatest failing is the lack of clear thinking about the role Poland is to play within NATO and about the military's new equipment needs and the future of the country's defence industry.'[46] For this observer 'The army is fully engaged in resisting being divided into a NATO compatible 'better army' and an 'inferior army' which will vegetate...[and] its main priority is to save as many jobs as possible.'[47]

At least part of the motivation for this resistance is a residual concern for a greater capacity for re-mobilisation in the face of territorial threats. Lack of political will to tackle the issue, however, is also in part due to the political and economic impact of closing military installations on the scale necessary for reform.

Similar issues surface in the area of procurement policy where the desire to balance political concerns and military needs has not always been well handled. For some critics Poland is too concerned to let political pressures dictate the way in which major procurement decisions are made to the detriment of both its established procedures and its international reputation. As one critic observes, 'Having established a procurement policy with a list of priorities as to what to acquire in what order, this is not always stuck to. An example of this is the recent procurement of the British howitzer. Thus the US would like to see a more transparent and orderly procurement process.'[48]

According to another commentator, because of this tendency, 'Western defence contractors such as BAe Systems or Lockheed Martin are growing increasingly frustrated at the lack of clear procedures and strategic decisions, which would allow them to tender bids to supply aircraft or other military hardware.'[49]

Other observers have expressed a similar concern about the forthcoming decision on the procurement of an advanced fighter aircraft for the Polish Air Force and the procedures by which this decision will be made.[50] The sacking of the Procurement Minister Romuald Szeremietiew in July 2001, in a scandal over alleged bribery, did little to boost confidence in this process.[51] As a Bush administration NSC member observed, 'we hope that if they want to buy an advanced fighter that they buy the F-16s. We would wish, though, that whichever purchase they make they do so on the basis of the merits of the aircraft and how it meets their needs, not the offset package of investment schemes that often go with such purchases and have little to do with defence policy.'[52] According to several commentators in Washington, it seems likely that Poland will not heed this advice in its aircraft choice. The likely decision in favour of the American F-16 will most probably be made on the calculation that this will draw Poland closer to Washington, rather than the merits of the aircraft, its price or indeed the offset deal.[53] Again it seems, even to the frustration of Washington, Poland's desire to seek a closer relationship with the United States pervades every aspect of policy.

Despite these criticisms Poland has made considerable progress in reforming its armed forces in line with NATO membership. It has already substantially reduced personnel levels from over 500,000 in 1988 towards the new goal of 150,000. While many obstacles need to be overcome as part of this process Poland is committed to having 30 per cent of its forces interoperable at NATO standard by 2006 as part of a six-year, 1.5 billion-dollar restructuring plan. As part of this plan defence modernisation spending is to rise from 12 per cent to 23 per cent of the budget by 2006.[54] By 2010 it plans to have equipped 150 multi-role combat aircraft with 'smart' weapons and to have fully reorganised its Air Force to operate in wings and squadrons, units compatible with its NATO allies. The Polish Navy will also be equipped with 60 surface combatants, two of which will be frigates obtained from the US Navy.[55]

Perhaps of greater importance still is Poland's commitment to continue its defence spending at just under 2 per cent of its growing GDP, well above the European NATO average (presently in decline). For these reasons combined, official criticism and concern with Poland's military reform programme within the United States and NATO remains muted. As Janusz Onyszkiewicz, head of Poland's national defence committee in parliament observes, 'The assessment we have had from Brussels is that our political integration has been a complete success, but in military integration much is left to do.'[56]

The NATO' Parliamentary Assembly's report was even less critical, praising Poland's 'considerable progress' in adjusting its armed forces to NATO standards.[57]

Indeed, what criticism there is in Washington stems in part from the realisation that were Poland better equipped its contribution as a loyal ally could be even greater. This expectation of reform and contribution is reflected in Simon's conclusion that, 'It is conceivable that Poland will more than match Spain and will become a serious NATO military contributor of security, enhancing the Alliance's military capabilities.'[58] Poland has achieved a record of reform and an expectation of continued progress that reinforces its position as a new model ally in the eyes of the Washington policy community.

Conclusions

In the space of 12 years the Republic of Poland has succeeded in uniting the actions of its government with the sympathies of its people in establishing a close political relationship with Washington. What is perhaps even more remarkable is that this transformation has been so complete. From its position as a member of a hostile military alliance in 1989, by 1999 Poland had become one of America's most loyal NATO allies. At a fundamental level these two states share a similarity of world-view with regard to international politics which inspires a deep sense of kinship. Poland seeks to make an international contribution both regionally and globally. As Foreign Minister Geremek set out to the Sejm in 1999, 'As international security increases and regional affairs stabilise themselves, and as Poland's international position improves, our foreign and economic policies must establish more ambitious goals and have wider geographic horizons.'[59]

It is an approach that Washington both shares and appreciates. Furthermore, on a whole swath of specific issues they also share common strategic goals. Poland's geopolitical position determines its approach to Russia and the newly independent states to its east. This ensures that on the question of NATO enlargement Warsaw is as enthusiastic as Washington is.

Similarly, on ballistic missile defence Poland was more inclined to move beyond the Cold War paradigm of deterrence thinking than many allies were, even before the terrorist attacks on America. It is also keen to work to ensure that this issue is not allowed to damage transatlantic relations.

On ESDP the genuine concerns which Poland fears are supportive and supported by the objections which Washington has raised to their development. The long-term evolution of the European project is a process that both countries approach feeling better for the support of the other.

Furthermore both states see the benefit in a shared approach to international intelligence, and the employment of peacekeeping. Although unequal in stature both allies benefit from these forms of cooperation, which also contribute towards the growing bonds of trust that exist between Warsaw and Washington.

Because of the power inequality between Washington and Warsaw the nature of the special relationship that exists between them is very different for each of them. As one of many of Washington's allies Poland benefits from America's provision of European security and international order.

For the US, however, the contribution that Poland provides as an ally is circumscribed not only by its more limited resources, but also by the international context in which that relationship operates. Thus while Poland now has a strong and special relationship with the US it does so in the context of America's other relationships. As a result, for example, Poland is unlikely to supplant Israel or Britain in the hierarchy of America's allies because the patterns of cooperation that exist with those powers are well established. (This is even more the case in the aftermath of 11 September 2001 when the military contribution of Britain and the security predicament of Israel have raised the profile of both these allies).

Nor is its greater loyalty to Washington than France or Germany going to outweigh the political significance of those states in America's diplomatic calculations. Even within a collective EU its ability to influence the course of events seems limited without the diplomatic cooperation of at least some of the major powers. Jeffrey Simon's comparison with the Spanish contribution to NATO is perhaps the most illustrative of the contributions which Poland can offer the alliance.

Military capabilities aside, however, Poland's role as one of the first in a series of new NATO members gives it an unusual role in its relationship with both Washington and NATO. It is in this sense that Poland can be considered by Washington as a 'new model' ally. Crucially for Washington, Poland is committed to be a security provider and not just a consumer. It has demonstrated a willingness to contribute actively wherever possible to peacekeeping operations, and it has set the standard in terms of resources committed and modernisation achieved in the process of defence reform. Its political support for the US both within Europe and globally has also been without question. In short it is a role model that Washington would like to see all subsequent new NATO members emulate.

While criticisms over the pace and scope of Poland's military reforms and frustrations over the state of its procurement procedures are often voiced in the US, substantial problems with Warsaw's role as Washington's new ally are hard to find. There are no major areas of disagreement. Even on social issues, an area that often divides America from its European allies, socially conservative Poland is often at one with the US.

The area which comes nearest to be an irritant for some in Washington's policy community is the residual concern that Warsaw has with the prioritisation of Article 5 security concerns over other roles and missions. Here again, however, American frustrations are motivated by a desire to see Poland fully embrace the twenty-first century security environment and to reconfigure its military and outlook accordingly.

What impact a continued reduction of concern with territorial defence would have on Polish-American relations, however, is also an important topic of speculation. This is the case, it is argued, since a more secure Poland would be a less eager ally to Washington. Following this logic, to persuade Poland that it was safe in NATO because of the American security guarantee would be one thing, to persuade Warsaw that it was no longer threatened could be quite another. While there might be some element of truth to this line of reasoning its mono-causal explanation for Poland's transatlanticism is not persuasive. Even on these terms, a Poland that felt secure to the East would still be eager to ensure American involvement in Europe as a balance to the potential domination of the EU by its largest member, Germany.

This line of reasoning also feeds into the speculation as to what effect Polish EU membership will have on the relations between Warsaw and Washington. On both sides of the Atlantic there is interest to see whether EU membership makes Poland more 'European' or whether membership makes the EU more Atlanticist. The notion that a choice exists between being a good European and a good Atlanticist, however, is an idea that Poland rejects a priori. For this reason Polish criticism of ESDP in a way that is supportive of American concerns, while at the same time as applying for membership of the EU, involves no contradiction. This approach, however, while popular in Washington is resented in some European capitals. As one senior EU diplomat in Warsaw remarked, 'There is no getting away from the fact that some countries perceive the Poles as having strongly divided loyalties.'[60]

The French in particular have voiced concerns that Poland's pro-Americanism could make it a virtual 'stalking horse for US interests within the EU'.[61] While some Americans hope that this approach will moderate elements of anti-American feelings within the EU, others fear that the desire to conform to the prevailing European ethos might result in Poland becoming a less supportive ally of America as an EU member. While this debate shows how close an ally Poland has become for the US, on the other hand Warsaw's utility to Washington will be limited if it is merely perceived as doing America's bidding in Europe. Such a position would be in neither Poland's nor America's interests.

That so much has been achieved in Polish-American relations in a short time is in part a reflection of the complementarity of strategic interests and worldview that exists between the two states. Such is the range of the common interests and political bonds between these new allies that the foundations of their relationship have become well established. The only possible challenge to that relationship could be the impact that EU membership for Poland will have.

This in turn is also subject to the impact that EU enlargement will have on the EU as an institution generally, and the success or otherwise of ESDP within the NATO alliance context. Even if Poland were to moderate its position between Brussels and Washington, however, this would still be to the net benefit of the United States. An EU with an active and internationally focused Poland as a member would be preferable to the US than one without. For Poland too, the ability to influence the way the EU acts internationally will also be preferable to its present exclusion from matters that directly affect its interests.

Similarly, if Polish support for the US internationally were to become less unconditional as a result of membership then this might also be to America's advantage. After all, international support for US actions, and the legitimacy that such support provides, is more credible when it is clearly seen as being an endorsement of the **act** rather than the **actor**.

In the final analysis, being a good ally at times also means knowing when to voice disagreement. Perhaps only when this stage is reached and the present honeymoon in Polish-American relations is over, will Poland truly be able to be considered America's new model ally. As America prepares for its 'phase two' in its 'war against terrorism' and the wisdom or otherwise of attacking Iraq is debated within the alliance and elsewhere, it may not be long before Poland has to decide what sort of model ally it will be within NATO.[62]

NOTES

I would like to thank Tom Timberman, Stuart Croft, Richard Lock-Pullan and Raymond Dunn for their helpful comments on an earlier draft of this article.

1. Bush added, 'I came here to show nations that are hungry for democracy or striving for democracy or looking at democracy, what's possible, and Poland serves as a bridge and an important example.' 'Text: Bush News Conference with President of Poland', www.washingtonpost...politics/bushpoland061501.htm, 15 June 2001.
2. Ibid.
3. 'A Commitment To Europe', Editorial, *The Washington Post*, 29 April 2001.
4. For as Howard observes, despite its longevity NATO has been an essentially 'unhappy successful marriage', held together by common purpose rather than emotional bonds. Michael Howard, 'An Unhappy Successful Marriage: Security Means Knowing What To Expect', *Foreign Affairs* 78/3 (May/June 1999) pp.16–27.
5. John Reed, 'Poland's US Ties May Leave It Out Of Step With New Partners: EU Membership is looming but Some States Are Suspicious Of Polish Foreign Policy Leanings', *The Financial Times*, 15 March 2001.
6. In a speech in London in 1982, for example, Reagan affirmed that Poland was at 'the center of European civilisation'. Fareed Zakaria, 'Could Russia Join The West?', *Newsweek*, 25 June 2001.
7. Ian Fisher, 'The US and Its Leader Are Popular With Poles', *The New York Times*, 16 June 2001.

8. Ronald E. Powaski, 'Joining The March of Folly', *The Bulletin of the Atomic Scientists* 54 (Jan./Feb. 1998).
9. See Reed (note 5).
10. Cited by Fisher (note 7).
11. Andrew A. Michta, 'Poland: A Linchpin of Regional Security', in Andrew A. Michta (ed.) *America's new Allies: Poland, Hungary and the Czech Republic in NATO* (Seattle: Univ. of Washington Press 1999) p.62.
12. See Michta (note 11) p.45 and p.63.
13. Przemyslaw Grudzinski, 'A View From Poland: What Now, Who Next?' in Simon Serfaty (ed.) *NATO at 50: What Now, Who Next, What Else?* (Washington DC: CSIS 1999) pp.11–12.
14. Sebestyen L. V. Gorka, 'NATO after enlargement: Is the Alliance better off?', *NATO Review* 47/3 (Autumn 1999) pp.33–35.
15. 'NATO Member Poland Offers Troops for Afghanistan', Reuters, 23 Nov. 2001.
16. Confidential interview, Washington DC. 2001.
17. 'NATO's Robertson to push new member Poland to overhaul forces', Deutsche Presse-Agentur, 29 March 2001. Lexis-Nexis.
18. 'Poland Sees NATO Peacekeeping Activities As Positive Evolution-Minister', BBC Monitoring Service, 30 July 2001.
19. Grzegorz Holdanowicz, 'Marynarka Wojenna sets new course for NATO integration', *Jane's Navy International* (Sept. 2001) p.35.
20. *Jane's Fighting Ships 2001–2002*, www.janes.com, p.534.
21. BBC (note 18).
22. See Gorka (note 14).
23. See Sabina A-M Crisen, 'NATO and Europe in the 21st Century: New Roles for a Changing Partnership', *The Wilson Quarterly* (Winter 2001).
24. '2 Polish Security Chiefs Quit', 25 Oct. 2001, <www.washingtonpost.com/wp-srv/apomline/20021025aponline>.
25. Elizabeth Williamson, 'Poland's President Kwasniewski Serves As A Conduit For East West Diplomacy', *The Wall Street Journal*, 20 Nov. 2001.
26. Interview, Washington DC.
27. See Michta (note 11) p.49.
28. Interview, CSIS, Washington DC, April 2001.
29. Confidential interview, Washington DC, April 2001
30. Ibid.
31. See the views of the American CATO Institute, for example, at <www.CATO.org>.
32. Confidential interviews with Senate staffers, Washington DC, April 2001.
33. See R.D.Asmus, R.L. Kugler and F.S.Larabee, 'What Will NATO Enlargement Cost?' *Survival* 38/3 (Autumn 1996) pp.5–25. A 1996 RAND study suggested that the cost could be as high as $100 billion.
34. See Michael E. Brown, 'The Flawed Logic of NATO Expansion', *Survival* 37/1 (Spring 1995) pp.34–52.
35. See Zbigniew Brzezinski, 'A Robust and Credible Process', in Serfaty (note 13).
36. Confidential interview, Bush administration NSC, Washington DC, April 2001.
37. Philip H. Gordon and James B. Steinberg, 'NATO Enlargement: Moving Forward', *Brookings Policy Brief* 90 (Nov. 2001) <www.brookings.org/comm/policybriefs.pb90.htm>.
38. Confidential interview with Senate staffer, Washington DC, April 2001.
39. See President Kwasniewski's comments in, 'It's a new system. It can be for all of us: NATO countries, other countries, including Russia and China.' Anton La Guardia, *The Daily Telegraph*, 16 June 2001.
40. Confidential interview.
41. 'Poland Sees NATO Peacekeeping Activities As Positive Evolution-Minister', BBC Monitoring Service, 30 July 2001.
42. Jeffrey Simon, 'NATO's Membership Action Plan and Defense Planning: Credibility at Stake', *Problems of Post Communism* (May/June 2001) p.33.

43. Jeffrey Simon, 'NATO's Membership Action Plan (MAP) And Prospects For The Next Round of Enlargement', *East European Studies: Occasional Paper 58* (Washington DC: The Woodrow Wilson Center, Nov. 2000) p.8.
44. Cited by Jeffrey Simon, 'Transforming the Armed Forces of Central and East Europe', *Strategic Forum* 172 (Washington DC: National Defence Univ., 2000) p.3.
45. Jeffrey Simon, 'The New NATO Members: Will They Contribute?', *Strategic Forum* 160 (Washington DC: National Defence Univ., April 2000) p.4.
46. Christopher Bobinski, 'Membership a Tough Test: NATO', *Financial Times,* 17 April 2000.
47. Ibid.
48. Ibid.
49. Confidential interview, Washington DC, April 2001.
50. See Bobinski (note 46).
51. According to a Clinton NSC member, 'Poland needs to learn to manage in a more routine way the pressures from certain EU countries to be better Europeans, to buy Mirage jets or whatever. It is not a choice that needs to be made with every purchase.' Confidential interview, Washington, DC, 2001.
52. John Reed, 'Poland on hold amid death throes of Solidarity government', *Financial Times,* 27 July 2001.
53. Confidential interview, Washington DC, April 2001.
54. Confidential interviews, Washington DC, April 2001.
55. Robert Anderson, *et al.,* 'NATO's newer members battle to upgrade their military punch', *Financial Times,* 11 July 2001.
56. Wojciech Luczak, 'Poland Details Future Defence Posture', *Military Technology,* Feb. 2000.
57. See Anderson *et al.* (note 55).
58. 'Poland made progress in adjusting armed forces to NATO, say NATO MPs', BBC Monitoring Service, 30 July 2001.
59. See Simon (note 44) p.4.
60. Statement by Foreign Minister Bronislaw Geremek to the Sejm, 8 April 1999. Cited by Wolczuk, in Wallace and Mayew (eds.), 'One Europe Or Several: Poland: A Partnership Profile', Sussex University Working Paper 4/01. See <www.one-europe.ac.uk>.
61. See Reed (note 52).
62. Ibid.

Security and Defence in the New Europe: Franco-Polish Relations – Victim of Neglect?

VANDA KNOWLES

In December 1998, France and Britain signed the declaration of Saint-Malo, marking a turning point in European efforts to construct a common defence policy. It clearly stated that the European Union (EU) should build the 'capacity for autonomous action, backed up by credible military forces'.[1] The significance of this event lies in the convergence it represents between the two European neighbours that previously occupied diametrically opposing positions on European security. Whereas Britain's 'special relationship' with the US has in the past secured its firm Atlanticist position in matters of security and defence, France has, for decades, championed the cause of a European defence. Saint-Malo and the rapid developments in the Common European Security and Defence Policy (CESDP) have again sharpened the debate on France's position within the transatlantic relationship and on the future of European security and defence in the context of an enlarging North Atlantic Treaty Organisation (NATO) and European Union.

The configuration of the 'New Europe' is fundamental to understanding European security and defence in the twenty-first century. Already a NATO member and a likely first-wave candidate to EU enlargement, Poland has an important role to play in this 'New Europe'. With the potential of becoming a significant 'security provider' in the future, Poland, a staunch ally of the US, sits with Britain at the Atlanticist end of the security and defence spectrum. Not only does this make the dynamics of Franco-Polish relations in this area particularly interesting, it also highlights the rather pressing need to address the apparent divisions and misconceptions that have come to dictate the current state of their relationship.

After a brief overview of Franco-Polish relations, this article will turn to French security and defence within the transatlantic relationship. It will then address some of the divergences in policy between the two countries, in particular within the context of ESDP, but also with regard to other issues at the heart of contemporary discussions on European defence, such as NATO enlargement and missile defence. The research for the article was carried out in the summer and autumn of 2001 and so does not cover developments that have taken place since 11 September and since the recent change of government in France.

France and Poland

Although the article deals principally with post-Cold War relations, it is essential to draw attention to the long-standing historical and cultural ties that exist between Poland and France, and the strong affinity exists between the peoples of the two nations. This has been strengthened by the presence of a considerable Polish émigré community in France. Another often cited illustration of this relationship is the massive engagement of the French society towards Poland during the period of martial law in the 1980s. French support for the Polish people resulted in pressure on the French government to stand behind the political opposition in Poland at the time. Despite the positive attitudes at the societal level, however, political relations since 1989 have at times been less propitious.

In the early 1990s there was considerable disappointment in Poland at the lack of French engagement in Central and Eastern Europe. President François Mitterrand was criticised for his lack of vision regarding the opening up of the eastern part of Europe. On EU enlargement he was perceived as being particularly hesitant, primarily due to the fear that 'widening' would come at the expense of any 'deepening' of the integration process, that Germany would have excessive influence in the region, and that the centre of gravity would shift towards the East and away from France. Mitterrand's proposal for a 'confederation' of states of the continent to include Russia but not the US and to replace the need to integrate the countries of the region into the European Community (EC), was rejected across the board. The Americans saw in it an attempt to marginalise them from Europe, and the states of Central and Eastern Europe wanted no part in an arrangement that involved Russia but excluded the US.

The election of Jacques Chirac as President in May 1995 has been described as a turning point in the history of bilateral relations, and 1995 is presented as a year in Polish-French relations 'in which we took advantage of the opportunities available to us and as a year which promises even better things to come'.[2] Indeed an opinion poll on 'Attitudes towards other nationalities: likes and dislikes' showed an increase from 51 per cent to 67 per cent in positive attitudes towards France from 1994 to 1995.[3]

Some see the roots of an improved relationship in the obvious support for EU enlargement shown earlier by Edouard Balladur as Prime Minister from 1993.[4] Nevertheless, the visit by President Chirac to Warsaw in 1996, where he mentioned the possibility of Poland joining the EU as early as 2000,[5] is widely regarded as a sign of a new impetus in Franco-Polish relations, following the reticence of the early 1990s. This visit was part of a two-year stretch of high diplomatic activity.

Since 1997, however, the tide has again turned and relations have become more problematic. One factor in the deterioration was undoubtedly the perception in Poland that France was supporting Romania over Poland as a candidate for NATO membership. Paris was insisting on the inclusion in the first wave of Romania and Slovenia, in addition to Poland, Hungary and the Czech Republic. Placing diplomatic weight behind Romania was perceived by the Poles as a French attempt to complicate and possibly prolong the process of enlargement.

The French denied this; their choice of candidate was due to strong traditional, cultural and linguistic ties as well as concern over the situation in the Balkans. Furthermore, it made no sense to compete with the head start Germany had already established in Central and Eastern Europe, and thus Paris adopted a strategy of cooperation and a division of roles.[6]

The return to power of a left of centre government in France, at a time when a centre-right coalition was in office in Poland, did not help to facilitate improved relations. At the same time, Polish foreign policy was arguably taking an increasingly Atlanticist direction in foreign policy. One possible manifestation of this was the joint US-Polish organised conference in Warsaw in June 2000 'Towards a Community of Democracies'. France was the only state of the participating 107 not to sign the 'Warsaw Declaration', claiming that the conference and the declaration itself promoted a model of democracy they did not believe in exporting universally. The rejection of the declaration was, nevertheless, interpreted as a result of French opposition to the US.[7]

The onset of the rather inauspicious period in Franco-Polish relations outlined above mirrors a similar cooling-down of relations between France and NATO, to which the article will now turn.

French Security and the Transatlantic Relationship

France has held a prominent place in the patchy development of a

European defence and, with the declaration of Saint-Malo in December 1998, undoubtedly retains a key role in the development of the continent's new post-Cold War defence and security structures. Indeed the 'position of France' has been described as one of four factors that, in various configurations, have determined European defence over the last 50 years. The other three factors being the commitment of the US to Europe, transatlantic relations, and the construction of Europe.[8] Within Western Europe, it was France's independent role within NATO that characterised much of the debate and led to the country becoming such an 'outlier' in matters of security and defence in Europe.[9]

The post-war strategic culture[10] in France was grounded on the need to recover some of the prestige the country had held and on a drive to re-establish and assert its great power status. At the same time, an obsession with independence and complete military autonomy were the result of bitter memories of having relied on 'Anglo-Saxons' for their security in World War II.[11]

It was the desire for complete military autonomy in particular that led General de Gaulle to withdraw France from NATO's integrated military structure in 1966.[12] To this day France is a member of the Atlantic Alliance but this remains 'alliance without integration'.[13] It was indeed during the de Gaulle period that French defence policy took on some of the characteristics that were to continue to mark it until the present day. The maintenance of an independent nuclear force along with the principle of national autonomous decision-making are two of the most prominent.[14]

The centre-right coalition headed by Edouard Balladur that came to power in March 1993 brought France closer to NATO structures and promoted fuller participation by France in NATO's political and military work, including a return to NATO's Military Committee.[15] More recently, in 1995, the then newly elected President Chirac quickened the pace of improved relations with NATO and took steps to reintegrate France into the Alliance's military structures. The rationale behind this was the belief that if a European defence policy were at all possible, it could only be achieved in concert with the European partners, the majority of which were inside NATO.[16] By recasting NATO in a more 'European' mould, France could assert more influence and voice from within than would be possible from the outside, which had been easier prior to 1989 when France still enjoyed a particular status. Given the firm Gaullist foreign policy foundations, and indeed his own Gaullist credentials, Chirac was aware that NATO would have to visibly 'Europeanise' for the French to accept reintegration into the military structures.[17]

For a while this did seem to be the case, with moves on the part of NATO to create a European face to the Alliance through initiatives such as the Combined Joint Task Forces. Similarly, the French defence reforms of 1996 have as their underlying principle, a more mobile, collective and European defence. The development of a professional army, immediately deployable and geared towards crisis management has considerably improved interoperability with NATO.[18]

However, disagreement over who should take charge of NATO's Southern Command led to stalemate. Paris concluded that the Alliance had not re-balanced itself enough. The final straw came at the Madrid summit in 1997 when the US announced its three candidates for NATO enlargement, which did not include France's preferred candidates, Romania and Slovenia. Any hope of a rebirth was completely scuppered in 1997 with the victory of the parties of the Left, headed by the Socialist Party (PS) with Lionel Jospin as Prime Minister. The new government was decidedly against any return to NATO structures.[19]

The events of 11 September 2001 undoubtedly leave the door open for yet another re-casting of the relationship between Europe and the US and also between France and NATO. Nevertheless, the purpose of the overview of both Franco-Polish relations and the position of France with regard to NATO is to provide the beginnings of an analysis into why Franco-Polish relations are less than propitious, particularly in matters of security and defence.

The next significant development was the signing of the Saint-Malo declaration. The initial Polish response to the development of a CESDP was one of reticence; anxious about the effect it might have on Euro-Atlantic relations.[20] This is not so surprising when one considers the timing of the declaration, hot on the heels of a particularly rocky period in post-Cold War Franco-American relations and indeed in French dealings with NATO. This left the situation open to the interpretation that France was in fact attempting to create a European alternative to NATO, despite the UK also being signatory to the declaration.

As far as Paris was concerned, the enlargement of NATO in 1999 to include the three new members, Poland, Hungary and the Czech Republic, tipped the balance of NATO even further towards US hegemony. France had not succeeded in securing first-wave places for Slovenia and Romania who, it had hoped, would have created at least some degree of counterbalance to the three decidedly pro-American Central European states.

Saint-Malo, in December 1998, and NATO enlargement in March 1999 brought both France and Poland to centre stage. With both keen to forge a role for themselves within their respective contexts, the extent of their actual discord on security and defence issues was perhaps made more visible and exaggerated as a result. The remainder of the article addresses the areas that appear to present the greatest sources of antagonism and, in particular, the role of rhetoric and political discourse in defining the parameters of the debate.

European Security and Defence Policy – Where do the problems lie?

While there has certainly been a change of tack since the mid 1990s, there is nevertheless a continuity in the consistent, underlying *finalité* to French European defence policy, which sits so uneasily with its European allies and that leaves it out on a 'European' limb in security and defence. As one high-ranking official at the Quai d'Orsay put it,

> It is very clear. Our long-term objective is to construct a European defence. But a European defence that goes beyond crisis management, a real defence, a real defence policy[21]

This is a fundamental point of difference between the two countries. Although France has never formally relied on the Alliance's defence guarantee, the Poles are firmly, some claim obsessively, tied to NATO's Article 5 in particular, and the territorial defence guarantee it provides. The country's turbulent history and tragic experience of invasion and occupation explain this stance very clearly. Paris may have no qualms about a European defence provided by Europeans, indeed may well prefer it. Warsaw, on the other hand, cannot envisage a European defence without the US.

France's desire to achieve a European defence policy stems partly from an obsession with anchoring Germany in European structures. Determination to maintain a European option faced with the post-war hegemony of the US in European defence also plays a role and has been the driving force behind the various failed attempts at launching a European defence policy. It is in defence and security policy that France sees an opportunity to play a key role in Europe.

While recent history has helped persuade the Europeans of the need for a European policy and capability in defence and security, Kosovo in particular highlighted the lack of capacity the Europeans have at the moment to act without the support of NATO. Given that the building up of a European capacity is not achievable in the short term, NATO remains indispensable. The French are as aware of this fact as the other European countries are. Any attempt to assert a European Security and Defence Policy and deploy a Rapid Reaction Force before it is ready will consign the whole project to an early grave, from which another resurrection would be practically impossible. Thus despite its desire to see the construction of a European defence, the wish to see NATO and thus the US continue to play a role on the European continent is clearly stated and upheld across the political spectrum in France.

> In this changed world, Europeans and Americans have common values and interests. They have the means of guaranteeing them. They will only achieve this on the basis of a balanced co-operation, rooted in dialogue and trust.[22]

The strength of these sentiments has certainly been magnified since the terrorist attacks on Washington and New York, and this will perhaps play a role in reconfiguring relations on a broader scale. Although recent concern voiced at the 'axis of evil' speech by President Bush, particularly by the then Foreign Minster Hubert Védrine, who referred to Bush's reasoning as simplistic[23] and criticised the unilateralism of the US, suggests the widening of an underlying rupture in European-US stances on the fight against terror.

Nevertheless, France has been frequently criticised, including in Warsaw, for systematically pursuing an anti-American policy in defence matters, symptom of the more broadly felt rejection of American hegemony, whether economic, cultural or political. Although there are some in France who do support strengthening Europe as a means of challenging this hegemony, including 'a few French Gaullists as well as left-wingers in many EU countries',[24] they do not necessarily constitute the majority view. Rather, the pursuit of what is often perceived as an ostensibly anti-American policy stems from a desire to *Europeanise* NATO and protect European structures from nato-isation: thus to re-balance NATO and not to create a counter-balance to the US. Paris has continued to assert that a more balanced and stronger Atlantic Alliance would be the result of an effective CESDP.[25]

Rebalancing or counter-balancing? Europe or America?

The perception of anti-Americanism remains, however, and highlights an obvious clash with Polish considerations in security and defence. Ties between Poland and the US date back much further than 1990, as the contribution by David Dunn clearly shows. However, since it emerged from behind the Iron Curtain and embarked upon its 'return to Europe', beginning with NATO membership, Poland has again become a player.

Geostrategic location, size, population, its sense of self and desire to forge a role for itself also make it a particularly significant player within the region and this will conceivably increase with EU membership. As already mentioned, the timing of events leading up to Polish NATO membership perhaps served to render its pro-Americanism more visible, particularly for Paris.

Extreme stereotypes of pro- and anti-Americanism have led to the creation and consistent application of a false dichotomy to the debate, which has served to form another point of contention for Polish-French relations: Poland having to choose between Europe and the US. The French strongly deny that Poland was ever asked to make this choice, as being a 'good European' is not incompatible with being a 'good NATO ally'. Indeed views expressed during the interviews carried out in Warsaw for this project also illustrate that the Poles do not regard this position as contradictory. Nevertheless Poland is perceived in Paris as systematically siding with the US, attempting to be the 'model pupil of the new NATO class',[26] along with the British, almost always supporting the American position within NATO.[27] This leads to frustration at the Polish inability to realise that voicing criticism does not necessarily make you a bad ally. For many, the way France has supported and participated in NATO operations provides clear proof of this.[28]

The fact that the NATO-Europe (or US-Europe) dichotomy is continually applied prevents the emergence of any more nuanced interpretation of the position. France, as well as perpetrating the crime, also suffers from it, as it is systematically characterised as promoting a European, or rather anti-US, policy. The mistrust of France that this position provokes in Poland is tangible. One Polish interviewee, when asked about a European force acting autonomously from the US, stated it would present no problem under British command, but would be out of the question if under French command.[29] The role of the US here is crucial. It has even been suggested that the US played a considerable role in portraying Saint-Malo as another French attempt at 'independence', with the intention of influencing Poland and the other new NATO members. Without addressing the need for a change in the stereotypical frame of rhetoric that is so detrimental to the process of formulating alternatives, any attempt at conducting a different kind of politics will be extremely difficult.

Autonomous Planning Capacity

A further point of contention has been the issue of independent planning capacity. This is certainly an area of ESDP that has aroused considerable apprehension in Warsaw and has been instrumental in increasing the divide between France and Poland. Again in this case the debate was infused by a series of maladroit statements made in the early days of ESDP over the meaning and significance of 'autonomous capacity'. The result was to set alarm bells ringing in many European capitals, and particularly in Warsaw, over the separatist undertones that seemed to be emerging from the French policy.

The French have been keen to clarify their stance following these incidents. Nevertheless oil had already been poured onto the flames. Several of the Polish officials interviewed for this project stated that although they doubted that the French were actually deeply anti-American and wanted NATO out of Europe, French rhetoric painted quite a different picture. Whether the initial statements were later retracted, reinterpreted or better translated, the fact remains that the original version had its impact on the debate, and unfortunately in each case simply helped amplify Polish fears.

French *finalité* in European defence policy, which is not shared by its European partners, explains in part the rather miscalculated remarks on autonomous planning capabilities that were so badly received. However, if the discussion is brought back to a level of capacity-building and 'pragmatisme', the options regarding planning capacities are relatively clear in Paris, and indeed the issues that initially caused concern and discord in this area have, to a large extent, been addressed and satisfactory solutions found.

There is no suggestion on the part of the Europeans that they take any independent responsibility for Article 5 collective defence. Despite this, the French long-term aspiration for a European defence policy would undoubtedly involve taking on responsibility for collective defence and not simply collective security. At the moment, however, where the 15 member-states would be prepared to act is in the carrying out of the Petersberg Tasks. For the moment the focus is on the development of a capacity that will allow Europe to tackle crisis management effectively without having to have recourse to NATO assets if the Alliance (effectively the US) decides it does not want to be involved.

> After all, that is our destination: the Common European Security and Defence Policy aims firstly and above all to strengthen our military capacities, with a view to improving the European contribution to their security and their continent, within the framework of the Alliance or within the framework of the EU.[30]

It is rather unlikely that in the near future such scenarios will arise; America is unlikely to refuse participation in an operation involving Petersberg Tasks. In essence, though, the French do not see a problem in EU operations without NATO assets. It would simply mean that national assets would be deployed instead of NATO assets. Britain and France are the two countries with planning capacities that could be utilised in such a scenario.[31]

It was stressed that the non-NATO assets option was particularly important for the development of a real European will to engage in crises. By systematising recourse to NATO in the first instance, the autonomy of the EU to act will automatically be reduced and it will be more difficult to mobilise public opinion and parliamentary support in favour of EU operations if NATO capacities for planning already exist.[32] For the French, this is an issue of the 'sovereignty of the 15' to have the right and ability to decide for themselves without NATO involvement. Whether the scenario then arises is almost irrelevant.

Where do They Stand in Contemporary Debates?

NATO Enlargement and Ostpolitik

Official French policy is in favour of further NATO enlargement and there is a firm consensus on the desire to avoid the public scandal of the first wave. As far as potential candidates are concerned, Slovakia and Slovenia present no threat to Russia and could easily be brought into NATO structures. There was a strong indication that the Baltic states, a stable region of no particular strategic importance to Russia, should all be taken in together.[33] One interviewee voiced concern that failure to do this might leave the door open for Russia to exert influence on its minorities in the remaining Baltic states, which could prove a dangerous destabilising factor.[34]

Reactions from Moscow are crucial in this respect. The belief that they key route to stability in the region runs via Moscow is a thread of continuity in French policy, according to the Defence Ministry.[35] Just as Poland has historically well justified reasons for its fear of Russia, France also has historical, traditional and geostrategic ties with Russia, which help explain its stance. During the de Gaulle period the President of the Republic did pursue a policy of détente with the then Soviet Union, culminating in a trip to Moscow in 1966.[36] This policy was later pursued by Presidents Pompidou and Giscard d'Estaing.[37]

Sympathetic French attitudes towards the USSR during the Cold War are remembered by many in Poland with distaste. Nevertheless, despite the conviction that everything should pass by Moscow in order to avoid deterioration in relations with Russia, the French clearly do not believe in leaving any power of veto with the Russians, particularly as regards future NATO enlargement.

Although there has been a recent improvement in Polish-Russian relations, paradoxically bolstered by Polish NATO membership, the burden of history continues to take a considerable toll. Polish policy has been dismissed in France as 'archaic geopolitics' and 'angoisse sécuritaire'[38] but nevertheless concern over Russia is a very real factor in the policy reasoning of the Polish state.

The rather pro-Russian undercurrent in the French position does constitute another deep divergence between Poland and French policies. One of the key issues here is that each has a very different view of who the important partners in the East are. Since 1990, Polish security policy has been firmly centred on a pro-Ukrainian position, advocating the continued and strengthened independence of that state from Russia. Whereas some French officials admitted it a weakness in the French position that there was no policy towards Ukraine[39] while underlining the importance of Russia, the Polish position is to treat Russia, Belarus and Ukraine as equal partners.

Important to note, nevertheless, is the rather more critical stance France has taken with regard to Russian policy in Chechnya. Russian military action in Chechnya is considered a grave mistake and France was one of the few countries to speak out publicly against the policy followed by Moscow. On this more sceptical view of Russia and President Putin a clearer rapprochement would perhaps seem possible between the French and Polish positions, than with Britain or Germany, for example, who were reluctant to address the issue of Chechnya. This has been understood as such by some in Poland, but has neither been widely acknowledged, nor exploited as one of few possible areas of convergence.[40]

European Union Enlargement

France's rather hesitant approach to EU enlargement has, at times, been read as opposition to the project. The view of those interviewed, however, was that this is not the case. They see French policy as having remained consistent, and simply more intellectually and politically honest than the approaches taken by some of its other European neighbours. Unlike them, it has not changed its discourse on enlargement in the last few years.[41] Enlargement was always regarded as a complicated and challenging process that would have to be negotiated and it was presented as such, without any false promises.

As far as the next wave of EU enlargement is concerned, provided that it proceeds objectively and on the basis of a true analysis of the accession negotiations, former foreign minister Védrine voiced his support for the 'big bang' option of letting ten new members join in 2004.[42] This option seems increasingly likely following the conclusions of the Commission's latest 'Regular Reports' on the progress of the candidate countries, which states that only Bulgaria and Romania can legitimately be left out of the first wave.[43] Védrine has, however, questioned whether, in this case, it would not make more sense simply to take in all 12 at once and has recommended careful consideration of the possible consequences excluding these two remaining states may have for the region.[44]

There is definite consensus on the role that Poland could play as a stabilising force in the region. The lack of any coherent French policy on Ukraine[45] means that Poland has a crucial role to play as a partner to France and its other European allies and indeed a 'bridge' between the EU and its eastern neighbours. A joint statement by the foreign ministers of France, Germany and Poland on the eve of the 10th anniversary of Ukrainian independence underscored 'Ukraine's importance as a European country' and expressed 'support for Ukraine's efforts towards rapprochement with European structures'.[46]

Missile Defence

French reactions to the US proposal to construct a missile defence system were initially rather vociferous. However, as one Quai d'Orsay official explained 'we do not like it but we have to live with it'. America has decided to go ahead with the project and so there is little point in creating confrontation, however much they dislike it.[47] Thus, like London and Berlin, Paris has decided to sit back and await the full panoply of options that will come with the project once it goes beyond the conceptual phase. When US experts made their tour of European capitals in May 2001, they were unable to answer the sorts of questions the French were eager to address. This far, it is difficult to effectively oppose something still so vague and theoretical.

Nevertheless, Hubert Védrine in particular took care to emphasise that, although they hoped to be consulted, a decision on missile defence was ultimately a sovereign American decision and that the Anti-Ballistic Missile (ABM) treaty involved America and Russia, even if the repercussions will be global. This could be in the hope that the US will take a similar stance on the sovereign decision of the '15' to construct an ESDP – in other words a project that the EU has decided to go ahead with, that the US probably does not like, but will have to live with.

Although Paris does not contest the changing dimensions of security and the dangers of ballistic proliferation, it does have a different view of the level of threat and the timescale within which it can actually evolve. The world has changed and the strategic balance has to be redefined, nevertheless there are fears that abandoning the ABM treaty would create a multipolarity that would leave the gates open to unbridled competition. Above all there is the view that it is up to Russia to give its view on the proposal.[48]

For Franco-Polish relations, missile defence has become yet another area where the two countries already find themselves on the diametrically opposing wings of opinion. After initial scepticism and concern over how Russia might react, Warsaw has since shifted to a position in favour of a missile defence that would also cover European partners. Indeed Polish territory has been offered as a base for the installations necessary for the project.[49]

A Future Together?

Having begun with a statement highlighting difference and conflict, it seems necessary to conclude with consideration of how far the two countries have come and where, and how, further convergence could be achieved.

The attitudes voiced in the French Ministry of Defence were much more sensitive to the evolution that had taken place in the Polish position, indeed it is seen to have evolved significantly particularly since the summits in Nice and Feira. During other interviews there was considerable criticism of the fact that Poland had failed to grasp two issues: on the one hand the magnitude of the civilisational changes that a 'return to Europe' would present to the incoming countries of Central and Eastern Europe, and on the other the psychological revolution confronting the current 15 in the conceptualisation and construction of the 'New Europe'. There is a visible change taking place, however, and undergoing the laborious process of accession to the EU has greatly improved Polish understanding of the European security and defence dossiers and has sensitised them to what is at stake in this area.[50]

Overcoming the 'either/or' dichotomy of 'Europe versus America and NATO' is fundamental to improved Polish-French relations in security and defence. There has been an evolution of both positions in recent months. The current focus on capabilities has helped considerably to detract attention from the more contentious debates. It was strongly voiced that what France most wanted to see was a more assertive Poland, which realises it can criticise without harming its reputation as a 'good ally'.

Also significant in overcoming this dichotomy is the choice and use of terminology. To present European intentions as 'autonomous defence' or 'independent defence' simply serves to muddy the waters when what is actually being proposed is a European capacity to maintain or re-establish peace within their own continent.[51] Systematic stereotyping of their positions, even if for effect, simply serves to consolidate these views as general perceptions and hampers the evolution of a more nuanced understanding. Particularly within the framework of ESDP and the transatlantic partnership, Polish-French relations would perhaps benefit from a more constructive dialogue if an effort were made to avoid terminology that imbues the situation with misunderstanding and antagonism.

It is crucial to underline the extent to which Polish accession to the EU will change many things. On the one hand this is true in so far as Poland will be able to oppose any plans the French might have for taking ESDP in a direction that conflicts with Polish interests. On the other, it will also change the nature of the framework within which Franco-Polish relations have been evolving over the last ten years. As a partner in Europe, Poland will begin to play the game of European politics with all the bargaining and package deals this involves. Agricultural policy is only one of many areas where France and Poland could find themselves in harmony. Such experiences will serve to build the trust that is visibly lacking in areas such as security and defence.

This brings us to *finalité* of French defence policy aspirations. Although the debate has been made less visible by the focus on capacity building, it will not disappear. To some extent, however, the fact that the French have a clear vision for the long term makes them easier to work with. Indeed, as was stated of French policy in the late 1980s, 'however ridiculous French strategic pretensions…may be, there is at least a discernible policy and set of objectives, even if they are unlikely to be achieved'.[52]

In any case, French aspirations towards a common European defence policy do not mean an end to NATO on the European continent. This is certainly not what the other 14 EU members want, and most importantly, does not seem to be what French policy is actually about. That one country believes in a European defence policy does not mean this will necessarily happen in the long term. That there is disagreement over the long-term aspirations should not give cause for suspicion and mistrust.

There are many similarities between France and Poland in the role perceptions they hold for themselves. As Philip Gordon explains, 'A national strategic culture with deep roots in history and geography is not easily abandoned.'[53] Criticism of Poland's obsession with Article 5 and its 'archaic geopolitics' inspired by its fear of Russia[54] have to be equated with the continued French apprehension at German parity within European institutions. For both countries, history can on occasions be the most decisive, and indeed obstructive, factor in policy decisions, often leading to positions more suited to the 'Old' rather than 'New' Europe.

Relations between the two countries are problematic particularly when a third party is involved; so far we have considered Russia and the US. Poland and France have both experienced difficult historical relations with their largest neighbour, Germany. They have nevertheless pursued successful paths of bilateral reconciliation with this important partner, despite the animosity that remains in historical memory. It is therefore all the more surprising that their own relationship, particularly in security and defence, remains so adversarial. Perhaps a clearer recognition is required of the fact that a problem exists and that the consideration of third parties has come at the cost of their bilateral relationship. A more proactive attempt and indeed will are required to overcome the current neglected state of relations, which is so far from the positive historical and cultural experiences that have characterised their past.

Finally, it is perhaps within the context of reconciliation that Franco-Polish relations might find a new impetus. The Weimar triangle has been of considerable symbolic significance since its conception in August 1991. More recently it has been criticised by many as symbolism of little substance or value when faced with the issues at the crux of accession.

For Poland it holds a continued significance, providing the country with a seat at the table with the two principle 'motors' of European integration. French attitudes have been more restrained. They range from general disappointment in what the forum has achieved in practice, to the view that Germany and Poland can now get on without France's help.[55] However it was also described by the former French foreign minister Védrine as one of the most intelligent and future-oriented initiatives in Europe.[56]

Furthermore, it should be recognised that this form of dialogue exists at various levels, and there was a much more enthusiastic appreciation to be heard at the French Ministry of Defence for the pragmatic achievements and potential future uses of the trilateral forum. In particular, it was stated that this was a forum where Poland had a voice, used it, and was listened to.[57]

With the Franco-German relationship also under pressure to prove its value as the source of dynamism in the New Europe, perhaps Weimar could provide the framework for a revitalisation of all three bilateral relationships. The troika embodies the dynamics of an enlarging Europe

102   POLAND

with a reconfigured set of interests and priorities. It certainly seems that it
could serve as a forum for discussion regarding the future *Ostpolitik* of the
EU, with Poland as a key player in the region. Again, this will require the
concerted effort of all to revive the institution's current status, but if
successful, perhaps it could prove instrumental as a cohesive force for
both the 'unhappy' couple and the 'neglected' one.

ACKNOWLEDGEMENTS

I would like to thank all those at the Quai d'Orsay, French Ministry of Defence and the Institut
Français des Relations Internationales, as well as the members of the National Assembly and
Senate who agreed to be interviewed for this article. The interviews were conducted in Paris in
May 2001. My thanks also go to Marcin Zaborowski, Adrian Hyde-Price, Michael Sutton and
Prof. Zdzisław Najder for their very valuable comments on previous drafts. Extracts taken from
interviews and speeches are my own translations

NOTES

1. Gilles Andréani, Christoph Bertram and Charles Grant, *Europe's Military Revolution*
    (London: Centre for European Reform 2001) p.11.
 2. Tomasz H. Orłowski, 'Relations with France', *Yearbook of Polish Foreign Policy* (1996)
    p.154.
 3. France ranked second highest after the US of those countries with which the Poles surveyed
    identified most positively. Germany ranked number 11, with only 35 per cent identifying
    positively with it in 1995. 'Sympatia I Niechęć do innych narodów', *CBOS Kommunikat
    Badań*, BS/173/99 (Nov. 1999).
 4. Michael Sutton, 'Chirac's foreign policy: continuity – with adjustment', *The World Today*
    (July 1995) p.138.
 5. Following a similar declaration by Chancellor Kohl the year before.
 6. Stanisław Parzymies, 'The Interests of Partners in Weimar Cooperation', *Central European
    Review*, 'The Weimar Triangle', 20–21 Feb. 1998, p.74.
 7. 'Francja przeciw deklaracji końcowej', *Rzeczpospolita*, 28 July 2000.
 8. Daniel Vernet,'Vers l'Europe de la Défense', *Commentaire* 23/92 (Winter 2000/1) p.780.
 9. Jolyon Howarth has also commented that despite presenting its defence and security as if
    acting for the whole of Europe, 'France's defence thinking on certain issues (nuclear policy,
    alliance policy, resourcing, industrial policy and conscription) has also been visibly out of
    step with the majority of its European partners', 'France' in Jolyon Howarth and Anand
    Menon (eds.) *The European Union and National Defence Policy* (London: Routledge 1997)
    p.23.
10. Described as a set of attitudes and policies towards defence and security that arises from
    history, geography and political culture. Philip H. Gordon, *France, Germany and the Western
    Alliance* (Boulder, CO, Oxford: Westview Press 1995) p.9.
11. Gordon (note 10) pp.9–10.
12. Important here is to consider the role of the Suez Crisis (1956) and the Cuban Missile
    Crisis (1962) in raising French doubts as to the reliability of the US as an ally.
13. Anand Menon, *France, NATO and the Limits of Independence 1981–1997: The Politics of
    Ambivalence* (London: Macmillan 2000).
14. Two of the nine elements highlighted by Philip Gordon as the basic guidelines that held
    for French policy-makers throughout the 1970s and 1980s that stemmed from Gaullist

principles, even though the actual policies themselves did change. Philip H. Gordon, *A Certain Idea of France: French Security Policy and the Gaullist Legacy* (Princeton UP 1993) p.164.

15. Gordon (note 10) p.85.
16. Vernet (note 8) p.781.
17. See Shaun Gregory, *French Defence Policy into the 21st Century* (Basingstoke: Macmillan 2000) Chapter 4, 'French Defence Policy in the New Europe'.
18. Speech by President Chirac to IHEDN, Paris, 8 June 2001, <www.elysee.fr>.
19. Vernet (note 8) p.781.
20. For more on the development of the Polish position see Olaf Osica, 'Common European Security and Defence Policy (CESDP) as seen by Poland', *Reports & Analyses* 5/01 (Warsaw: Centre for International Relations 2001) <www.csm.org.pl>.
21. Confidential interview, Quai d'Orsay, Paris, May 2001.
22. President Jacques Chirac, Special Meeting of the North Atlantic Council, Brussels, 13 June 2001. From site of the French President, <www.elysee.fr>.
23. Victor Mallet, 'The French Disconnection', Comment & Analysis, *Financial Times*, 26 Feb. 2002.
24. Andréani, Bertram and Grant (note 1) p.7.
25. Jolyon Howorth, 'European integration and defence: the ultimate challenge', *Chaillot Papers* 43 (Nov. 2000) p.2.
26. Confidential interview at Quai d'Orsay, Paris, May 2001.
27. Confidential interview at French Ministry of Defence, Paris, May 2001.
28. Confidential interview at Quai d'Orsay, Paris, May 2001.
29. Interview conducted on behalf of the project at Polish Ministry of Foreign Affairs, Department of European Security, Warsaw, Feb. 2001.
30. Speech by Alain Richard, French Minister of Defence, at the 'Wehrkunde', Munich, 3 Feb. 2001. <www.diplomatic.gouv.fr/europe/politique/defense/richard03020.html>.
31. Confidential interviews at Quai d'Orsay and Ministry of Defence, Paris, May 2001.
32. Confidential interview at French Ministry of Defence, Paris, May 2001.
33. Ibid.
34. Ibid.
35. Ibid.
36. Gordon (note 10) pp.14–15.
37. Frédéric Bozo, *La politique étrangère de la France depuis 1945* (Paris: La Découverte 1997) pp.61–71.
38. Confidential interview at Quai d'Orsay, Paris, May 2001.
39. Interviews at Quai d'Orsay and Senat, Paris, May 2001.
40. Interview conducted on behalf of the project with Prof. Zdzisław Najder, Warsaw, Feb. 2001.
41. Hubert Védrine interviewed by Polish press, Paris 14 March 2001. Ministère des Affaires Étrangères, Bulletin d'Actualités, 54/01 (16 March 2001). From site of French foreign ministry: <www.diplomatie.gouv.fr>.
42. General Affairs Council, Press Conference with the French Foreign Minister Hubert Védrine, Brussels, 19 November 2001. From the site of the French Foreign Minstry, <www.diplomatie.gouv.fr>.
43. Heather Grabbe, 'Heading for a Big Bang' (London: Centre for European Reform ,13 Nov. 2001).
44. General Affairs Council (note 42).
45. Confidential interviews held in Paris, May 2001.
46. RFE/RL Newsline, Part II, 22 Aug. 2001, <www.rferl.org>.
47. Confidential interview at Quai d'Orsay, Paris, May 2001.
48. President Jacques Chirac, Speech to the IHEDN, Paris, 8 June 2001, <www.elysee.fr>.
49. 'Polska zgoda na tarcze', *Rzeczpospolita*, 26 May 2001.
50. Confidential interview, French Ministry of Defence, Paris, May 2001.
51. François de Rose, 'Tensions euro-américaines', *Commentaire* 91 (2000) pp.745–6.
52. André Brigot, 'A Neighbour's Fears: Enduring Issues in Franco-German Relations' in

104 POLAND

ilippe G. Le Prestre (ed.) *French Security Policy in a Disarming World* (Boulder, CO and London: Lynne Rienner 1989) p.103.
53. Gordon (note 14) p.185.
54. Confidential interview at Quai d'Orsay, Paris, May 2001.
55. Ibid.
56. 'Polsko-Francuskie Stosunki Dwustronne', from the site of the Polish Foreign Ministry, <http://msz.gov.pl/bilateralne/pol_francja.html>.
57. Interview at French Ministry of Defence, Paris, May 2001.

The German-Polish Security Partnership within the Transatlantic Context – Convergence or Divergence?

KAI-OLAF LANG

Perhaps it was the Helsinki summit of December 1999 that showed clearly for the first time that the 'double Eastern enlargement' of the European Union (EU) and the North Atlantic Treaty Organisation (NATO) would not only plough up Europe's security landscape but also shift the balance of forces within the transatlantic community in a very specific way. When the three new NATO members voiced sharp criticism and reservations concerning the form and content of the new Common European Security and Defence Policy (CESDP) many European observers felt confirmed in their fear that, with the former communist countries of eastern central and south-eastern Europe, they had taken into the boat determined sympathisers of the American cause. After a short time, it came clear that Poland in particular would be an intransigent partisan of the US, criticising all forms of perceived European independence in security policy matters.[1]

In Germany, the Polish attitude was greeted with little enthusiasm even though Germans reacted in a more dispassionate manner than their French friends.[2] Still, a new constellation manifested itself for the first time: With regard to a strategic security policy question, Germany found itself between France, exponent of a pro-European orientation, and Poland, an uncompromising representative of NATO's exclusivity or at least supremacy for Europe's security and defence. The result is a rather sensitive situation because of the overriding importance German foreign policy attributes to bilateral relations both with France and Poland as well as to trilateral relations with both partners.

One may ask whether the disputes over the CESDP are not a sign of deeper discrepancies, which could affect Poland's relationship towards its western neighbour. Or to put it more dramatically: Do Poland's security policy objectives differ substantially from the German ones? Is it possible that Warsaw's priorities will eventually undermine the German-Polish security partnership that is both a condition and a result of an unprecedented improvement of the atmosphere between the two states after 1989?

The transatlantic relationship will remain a key element of any future development. The promotion of the CESDP, and thus the desire to affirm Europe as a political power with global reach through a common foreign and security policy, has clearly revealed that European positions vary a great deal. That the European Union is currently trying to find its own identity and its specific responses to globalisation, makes the situation no easier. These new circumstances have produced new challenges as well as new tensions in transatlantic relations.

Together with European integration, it was the orientation towards America that has constituted the foundation of German foreign policy in the four decades after World War II. It is with a mixture of careful attention and uncertainty that the country observes the above-mentioned new developments within the transatlantic community. The election of George W. Bush as the new US president and his administration's first declarations and steps were met with reactions ranging from criticism to concern. German political observers believed that the US would reduce its global military commitment, that the European allies would be asked to increase their defence contribution and that American foreign policy would adopt a 'tougher' stance towards China and Russia.[3]

The central long-term problem, however, is seen in a growing gap with regard to 'cultural' issues. In this respect, German foreign policy-makers are mostly concerned by two sorts of arguments.

First, the Euro-Atlantic partnership is bound together by common strategic goals on a global level as well as by common values outweighing differences between both sides.[4]

Second, tendencies aspiring to building a more self-confident Europe and the maintenance of the transatlantic Alliance are complementary developments.[5] All in all, Germany seems to aim at establishing a transatlantic relationship strengthened by a new internal equilibrium.

In the long run, the events of 11 September 2001 will not modify this perception. With Chancellor Gerhard Schröder advocating 'unlimited solidarity' with America and Germany actively supporting the US-led anti-terrorism-coalition Berlin and Washington seem as close as in the 'good old times' of German-American-Friendship. Nevertheless, relatively soon after the terrorist attacks criticism of the 'new closeness' to

America was voiced. The assumption of one German observer, according to whom 'there will be transatlantic dissonances before war is over',[6] is characteristic of what many think in Berlin: The problems that had existed before 11 September simply have not vanished. Moreover, for most German politicians and foreign policy experts it was clear from the very beginning that the fight against terrorism could not be a 'functional equivalent' for the fight against communism, which means that it cannot serve as a new transatlantic tie strong enough to minimise all other misunderstandings and conflicts.

The mainstream of Poland's foreign policy-makers traditionally want an Atlanticism 'without attributes'. That is why for them an approach of stabilising transatlantic relations by searching a new equilibrium in transatlantic relations is full of risks. This is especially the case because it is unclear whether Europe acts according to the principle 'as much of America as possible and as little of Europe as necessary' or vice versa 'as much of Europe as possible and as little of America as necessary'. Will this be dynamite for German-Polish common security policy interests?

First answers can be given by explaining German as well as Polish positions, objectives and expectations in key areas of security policy in the transatlantic context. At first, the attitudes concerning the Common European Security and Defence Policy (CESDP) will be dealt with, followed by other key questions in the transatlantic debate: the understanding of Article 5 of the North Atlantic Treaty, Poland's reform of the armed forces, the American anti-missile shield, the next NATO enlargement and Poland's policy towards the east. To conclude, the author will try to answer the question whether converging or diverging tendencies will dominate the security policy relationship between Germany and Poland.

Common European Security and Defence Policy (CESDP)

Germany's 'basic objective' regarding CESDP is to develop 'a European Union at the side of NATO', a Union 'strong in the field of security policy' and 'capable to act in military terms' to meet the challenges of the twenty-first century.[7] In consequence, by advocating Poland's accession to the EU Germany is not interested in a future member who harbours strong reservations against the long term project of creating a more active European security policy. In view of the resolute French commitment to the CESDP, a permanent hostile Polish attitude in this question would put Germany in an uncomfortable position between a strongly 'pro-European' and an equally strongly 'Atlanticist' partner.

Germany has therefore tried to make concessions to Polish demands to be included into the CESDP's new structures. However, the then German Defence Minister Rudolf Scharping made it absolutely clear that Germany subjects its promise of inclusion to EU competence – meaning that due to formal reasons non-members can not and will not be made part of EU decision-making processes.[8] A somehow acceptable solution was found in spring 2000 when a supplementary framework for the EU and the six EU candidates was established.[9]

It is true that Poland is not completely satisfied with the manner in which it is involved. Apart from 'consultations and dialogue' the country wants, according to Foreign Minister Bartoszewski, 'real cooperation'. Although the clarification process has softened Warsaw's dramatic responses, it has not eradicated its considerable scepticism towards the CESDP altogether. After all, it is not the mechanisms of participation for which Poland fights but the preservation of America's political and military commitment in Europe. In this context, in the eyes of Poland CESDP could insert a wedge into the Euro-Atlantic community. Poland's basic fear is that CESDP's *finalité* could erode the 'primacy of NATO'.[10]

However, it is exactly in this question about CESDP'S final destination where Germany and Poland have more in common than it could be expected at first glance. For the 'new' Federal Republic, too, the transatlantic link and the alliance with America will undoubtedly remain a key element of its foreign policy. Europe's integration is not regarded as the creation of an alternative, but as a project compatible with and complementary to transatlantic co-operation.

To effectively convince Warsaw of the CESDP's necessity Germany needs to make clear that searching for a 'new Atlanticism' with the US as guarantor of 'democracy, stability and economic prosperity' does not mean abandoning protection against common outside threats.[11]

Poland, on the other hand, would be well advised to take note of the fact that for Berlin the CESDP is no end in itself but considered to be essential for making Europe an active foreign political player. Thus, Warsaw should take into account that Germans also see CESDP as a project conducive to the creation of an integrated or federal Europe.[12]

NATO: Article 5 and Poland's Emphasis on Collective Defence

One can hardly resist the impression that, for quite a long time, political circles in Germany were voicing only vague opinions concerning the notion of NATO's internal solidarity in the post-Cold War era. A new international 'security environment' and the debate on NATO enlargement in the 1990s have initiated a slow but real change of consciousness. Diplomatic as well as military circles in Germany have increasingly come to the conclusion that NATO's successive enlargement and especially its 'penetration' into zones of political, ethnic and social instability would lead to a 'wider' interpretation of Article 5 of the North Atlantic Treaty.

It has to be emphasised that, even at a time of greatly reduced risks of major military strife in Europe, Germany maintains now as before the principle of mutual military assistance within the Alliance. Crisis prevention and crisis management are seen as new and additional duties which must not be fulfilled at the cost of NATO's 'traditional mandate'. There is no question that the new tasks will lead to a reorientation of security policy and restructuring of the military apparatus. The question is rather how far this shift of emphasis must go and how to implement the details.

In the days after the terrorist attacks, NATO, invoked the collective defence clause of Article 5 for the first time, producing more confusion than clarity about the meaning of mutual solidarity. The general impression from the German debate was that of a certain tendency towards a stronger 'politicisation' or even 'symbolisation' of the Alliance. At the same time, there was an inclination in Poland to understand NATO's mutual support as a system of very direct assistance, including military support. Statements of spontaneous support on the part of some Polish politicians according to whom Poland after 11 September was – just like the US – in a state of war, illustrated how far many some in Warsaw were prepared to go to show their solidarity.

In sum, Poland's preference for a more traditional interpretation of Article 5 has not led to greater political debates in Berlin. One of the reasons for this is certainly Poland's presence in the Balkans, by which Warsaw has demonstrated its willingness to be part of the Alliance's 'modern' activities. Furthermore, many observers in Berlin believe that Poland's NATO membership will eventually reduce the country's 'exaggerated' security needs.

Furthermore, after a relatively short time, in the wake of 11 September the basic reason for Poland's insisting on a narrow interpretation of Article 5 – the fear of Russian threat – has lost relevance. Of course, it would be too early to talk about a fundamental swing of opinion in Poland.

Altogether, the debate about the future of NATO, initiated by 11 September has not caused an increase of tensions between Germany and Poland. On the contrary, at the end of 2001 Germany and Poland found themselves belonging to the same 'camp' of NATO members that are rather cautious towards the transformation of NATO and the inclusion of

Russia.[13] Poland's demands – no veto power for Russia in NATO, no blockage of NATO enlargement by Russia, no marginalisation of Ukraine – are also supported by Germany (except for the stress on Ukraine). Despite sporadic statements in favour of Russia's NATO membership, the overwhelming majority of German politicians are very sceptical about the idea. Politicians, military leaders and experts rather sympathise with Minister Scharping's concept of an intensified cooperation with Russia excluding membership.[14]

Reform of the Armed Forces

In the medium and long term German foreign policy-makers expect that all new NATO members will eventually become 'producers of security". To this end, it is indispensable to build efficient, Alliance-compatible armed forces. As the only NATO member sharing borders with Poland, Germany was predestined to establish solid relations with the Polish armed forces and later, when Poland was soon to become a NATO member itself, to contribute to the harmonisation of the Polish Army and overall defence system with Alliance requirements.[15]

The restructuring of Poland's defence system to attain compatibility with NATO structures is not only a task of enormous proportion but is also complicated by the fact that the security environment itself is in a process of fundamental change. The military clashes in the Western Balkans during the 1990s have acted as a catalyst: they illustrate just how important it was that European NATO members solve the structural and functional problems of their armed forces and improve military capabilities.

According to the Federal Ministry of Defence, the main problem of the German *Bundeswehr* is its fixation on territorial defence, whereas what is required is its profound transformation into armed forces capable of multinational operations is required.[16] It is therefore deemed necessary to have, among other elements, highly qualified and motivated personnel, mobile and sustainable units for rapid deployment and multiple tasks, a competent and efficient leadership for multinational operations and modern and interoperable armament and equipment. At the same time, German military experts advocate common guidelines for the development of the Alliance's armed forces: step by step reduction of armed forces and of compulsory military service in order to be able to get the most modern army with a fixed defence budget.

According to German expectations, the profile described above is in principle also appropriate for Poland. To what extent does Poland's reform of the armed forces correspond to German views? It is impossible to give a final answer now, as the reform process has not yet come to an end. Nevertheless, there are a few indisputable points that should be mentioned here.

First, the perception of the Polish military has improved considerably as the Polish six year plan for the modernisation of its armed forces is regarded in Berlin as a feasible and financially viable concept which marks a clear improvement compared to the political zigzagging of previous years.

Second, there are good chances for German-Polish contacts in procurement and armaments cooperation. The German involvement in the modernisation of Poland's tanks (Leopardisation)[17] – which at the beginning of 2002 seemed to become more and more likely – could have symbolic meaning.

Third, Poland's willingness to participate in multinational units either together with eastern neighbours (POLLITBAT, POLUKRBAT) or with NATO partners (Corps North-East) is highly appreciated. In this context, observers have stressed that Poland's determination to get involved in 'confidence building' projects is so strong that even historical and domestic policy considerations recede into the background.[18]

Fourth, to German observers, the Balkan missions have revealed much about the state of the Polish Army. The quality of its soldiers, their capabilities and motivation are highly respected while the 'material framework' is considered problematic. In view of this, there is a widespread impression that Poland possesses above all one military trump card – namely 'cheap and decent soldiers'.[19] Therefore, many in Berlin believe that in the framework of an international military 'division of labour' Poland can make significant contributions, especially to the crisis reaction forces, depending not least on well trained and flexible personnel reserves.

There are, however, some voices of dissent from Poland to a one-sided orientation of their army to crisis reaction capacities.[20] Deriving from the country's NATO bordering status, it is argued here, a focus on territorial defence capabilities should be given a clear priority. However, Berlin does not expect Poland to concentrate on crisis reaction exclusively. Informed sources confirm that great importance is attached to Poland's ability to defend itself and to be a reliable partner when it comes to national and allied defence.

Missile Defence

Ever since the United States envisioned the creation of an anti-ballistic missile defence shield, Germany has been concerned that this could lead to a new arms race; to zones of different levels of security within NATO, growing antagonism between the US and Russia or China and in the end even to Europe's political alienation from America. It soon became clear that opposition from its European allies would not lead Washington to abandon its plans.

In Germany, Washington's firm stance brought about a differentiation of positions ranging from scepticism or even hostility to more flexible views. The opposition had always displayed profound understanding for the American project. In consequence, the Christian Democratic Union (CDU) and its Bavarian sister party (CSU) even advocate German participation in the anti-missile shield.[21] At the same time, there were voices even within the CDU saying that the (National) Missile Defense's main objective was to make America invulnerable so that it could 'dominate the world'.[22]

The range of opinions within the government coalition was even broader. Originally, it flatly rejected missile defence. An unexpected turnaround occurred when Chancellor Schröder declared that Germany was keeping an open mind. Due to economic and technologic-political motives, he added, Germany should not be fundamentally excluded from the project.[23] For the SPD's left wing and the majority of the Greens, however, the American anti-missile defence is unacceptable due to both technological feasibility and its consequences for defence and security policy. It remains to be seen whether these early differences will bring about a fundamental change of direction in this question.

In any case, German concerns are in sharp contrast to the uncritical reception with which the American plans were greeted in Poland. Leading Polish politicians have unanimously declared to be in favour of an anti-missile defence as long as it included all NATO allies.[24] In Brussels, the Polish Chief of Staff General Czesław Piątas claimed that Poland was prepared to allow missile defence installations on its territory. Also Poland's Defence Minister Bronisław Komorowski agreed and found it hard to imagine that, in the event that missile defence was realised there would be no elements of it in Poland.[25]

This ostentatious support for missile defence was hardly noticed in Germany. After all, no one believed Poland would play an outstanding role in the debate of this problem. Informed circles, however, were shaking their heads. Given the Polish defence sector's financial problems, the cost intensive installation of missile defence components would deal a heavy blow to the modernisation plans of the armed forces.

Another German criticism of Warsaw's behaviour points to the effect it could have on the period of détente in Polish-Russian relations that started in 2000.[26] Poles demanding their country's participation in America's missile defence system in order to provide protection against Russian nuclear missiles allegedly deployed in Kaliningrad[27] could give additional fuel to such German scepticism.

NATO Enlargement

For Poland the admission of three new members to NATO in 1999 has always been just one step in the process of the Alliance's further enlargement to the East and Southeast. Immediately after Poland's accession to NATO the Polish Presidential Office explained that even the mere question 'whether or not' there should be a second NATO enlargement was wrong: In view of the 1999 Washington decisions it was clear that NATO had to be open to other countries wishing to enter the Alliance and that only the 'when' and 'who' could be discussed.[28]

Similar views were voiced already at the end of 1999 by political parties as well as by officials in Warsaw's ministries of foreign affairs and defence. Poland's two direct neighbours, Slovakia and Lithuania, as well as the other Baltic states are topping the list of candidates Poland wants to see admitted into the Alliance as soon as possible.[29]

Berlin is not very enthusiastic about Warsaw's active role but reacts with benevolent understanding rather than sharp rejection. Apart from that, Germany's leading security policy squad does not seem to be mentally aware of the fact that Poland (and other 'new' NATO members) are indeed sitting at the table where basic strategic decisions are being made. This was illustrated by a leading German defence politician who explained as late as spring 2001 that until then, no NATO member state had clearly voted for another enlargement, a statement that – at that time – might be true for the 'old' members but certainly not for the 'new' ones.

It is useful here to give a brief overview of the German position on NATO enlargement. Since the end of 2000 a lively political debate on the process has taken place, including unambiguous positions. Nevertheless, a consensus was reached that quite soon, namely at the Prague summit in November 2002, some form of enlargement should take place. Moreover, Slovenia and Slovakia (of course, provided that the populist Vladimír Mečiar does not win the elections) are increasingly regarded as 'unproblematic' candidates. As to the rest, in 2001 almost everything appeared to be possible from Berlin's point of view. Particularly the debate on the sensitive issue of the Baltic states, and thus relations to Russia, runs across partisan lines. Be that as it may, it cannot be overlooked that, until autumn 2001, the German side had given no positive but also no negative signal concerning the Baltic states' NATO membership.

Summing up, the following divergences in Polish and German attitudes to NATO enlargement can be discerned:

After the first NATO enlargement, Germany did not see an urgent need to step forward and propagate another enlargement. With the accession of its two direct neighbours to the east, namely Poland and the Czech Republic, Germany was no longer the geostrategic frontier of the Alliance. This is now Poland's position. It is therefore in Poland's interest to change this situation – at least in part, by having Lithuania and Slovakia join NATO.

Berlin reflects NATO enlargement in terms of costs and benefits to a greater extent than Warsaw. From the German point of view, such an analysis based on security and military benefits comes up with no particularly positive results. Hardly anything promises to neutralise the risks of importing the internally fragile and externally crises-prone countries of the second round or an eventual deterioration of relations with Moscow caused by enlargement.

In Poland's view, Russia must not be allowed to block an eventual NATO enlargement, not even concerning the Baltic states. Although Germany does not accept a Russian veto either, it is, however, more prepared to 'take into consideration Russia's views'.[30] One of the principles advocated by the German government, namely the question whether or not 'the admission of a new state serves security and stability in Europe', can be understood as a fallback formula in case of Russian intransigence.

As far as the Baltic states are concerned it is a rather popular idea in Germany to offer them admission into the EU and to treat their inclusion into the mechanisms of CESDP as a substitute for NATO membership.[31]

Germany, Poland and the East

Poland intends to play an important role in creating the future Eastern policy of the European Union and the relations of the West to Russia and other countries of the former Soviet Union. As a Central European 'medium sized power' belonging to NATO and soon to the EU, Poland wants to exert influence on Europe's 'eastern dimension'.[32] As a pioneer of the reform process in post-communist Europe, Poland has been seen in Germany since the early 1990s as a leader in exporting stability, transferring security and projecting prosperity to the east.

Germany's growing willingness to accept Poland as a key actor in shaping the development in Eastern Europe conditions is a relatively new and certainly not irreversible development. Two factors, which became visible at the end of the 1990s, have changed Germany's perception.

First, looking at the prospects of an enlarged European Union, Germany became aware of the fact that the countries on Poland's eastern borders would be very much affected by the expansion of the Union.

Second, the fragile situation in Ukraine has attracted greater attention to this colossus on feet of clay.

Most German observers believe that Poland is especially competent to deal with the countries to its east due to geographical proximity, historical links, its economic, personal, cultural and political contacts. Especially with regard to Ukraine – which had long been neglected in German considerations on the 'East' – Germany is counting on Polish assistance.

On the other hand, Berlin is not all that happy to hear Warsaw's eternal lamentations concerning the lack of European engagement in favour of Ukraine, while praising US policy. Here, German observers point out that EU financial aid for Ukraine is substantially higher than that of the Americans. It is true, however, that German foreign policy shows little enthusiasm to offer Ukraine any prospect of EU membership[33] and that, in general, there is a tendency to think about Ukraine only in the context of Russia.[34]

If Poland wants to consolidate its status as Berlin's privileged dialogue partner and become a permanent multiple interface 'with the East' it has, first of all, to bring its policy towards Russia in agreement with German and EU expectations.[35] Germany envisages 'Russia taking an active role' within a 'differentiated framework'[36] and intends to intensify security policy cooperation in the framework of NATO-Russia cooperation and within OSCE. At the same time it is putting great hopes on the dialogue between Russia and the EU.[37]

As recent years have shown, it is in this field where contradictions between German expectations on the one hand and Polish calculations on the other could be observed. It is true that in many areas of cooperation with Russia European objectives coincide with Polish ones, such as the future EU enclave Kaliningrad, the Baltic Sea Council or the regional cross-border cooperation including Russian communities and areas. Still, substantial frictions concerning the policy towards Russia have occurred. Poland's resolute attitude towards Russian operations in Chechnya, quarrels about the presence of Russian secret service personnel in Poland and not least unresolved questions concerning the recent history between both countries show that bilateral relations between Poland and Russia are anything but stable.[38]

Of course, during 2001 the Russian-Polish relationship has changed significantly. A lively diplomatic exchange has melted the ice between

Warsaw and Moscow. Already in spring 2001, the Duma President Giennadiy Syeleznov proclaimed in Warsaw that the crisis in Polish-Russian relations had been overcome.[39] President Vladimir Putin's visit to Poland in January 2002 showed that a completely new mood prevails in Polish-Russian relations. Poland's new attitude seems determined by an unemotional assessment of its own interests in the European context, by a new objectivity due to NATO membership, a realistic perception of Russia and a cautious approach to problems resulting from the past.[40] This new pragmatism was made possible by Russia's new behaviour within a bilateral context and its interest in intensified cooperation with the EU and NATO.

However, it would be too early to speak of a breakthrough. Poland continues to be sceptical about any hasty intensification of economic and political contacts – also with regard to EU contacts with Russia. Poland is very attentive to the fact that cooperating with Europe means for Russia (also) to reinforce Europe's 'anti-American' direction.[41]

In Germany, such worries hardly exist. Here, there has been some fear that Poland will be a partner who would rather follow the American line when dealing with Moscow, that is, a line 'of benign neglect', [while] the majority of Europeans opt for critical cooperation'.[42]

All in all, we can say that from the German point of view, Poland will bring to bear its potential in Eastern policy only when its relations with Russia run parallel to the EU's objectives. If Poland succeeds in defusing the sharp contrast in its attitudes towards Ukraine and Russia it could define itself not so much as a 'bastion of the west' but rather as a 'bridge to the east'.[43] In this sense, the debate on Poland's eastern policy and on a possible readjustment of the 'strategic partnership' with Ukraine as initiated at the end of 2000 is promising.[44]

Conclusions: Prospects of German-Polish Security Partnership

Since the mid-1990s, Germany has become one of Poland's most favoured international partners. The public perception not only sees Germany as the most desirable partner for political cooperation and economic contacts but also regarding military relations Germany ranges high on the list of preferable partners.[45] This classification in public opinion, however, is less the result of a special love for the western neighbour but rather stems from a sober assessment of cooperation potentials and the situation of European interests.[46]

It also contrasts with the views of a large majority of the Polish political elite which orients itself towards the US. The question is whether or not by such a posture Poland's foreign policy establishment risks sacrificing its European interests for ideologically motivated Americanophile reflexes, at the same time putting stress on its relations with its western neighbour. The answer is: in the short term no, in the medium term, probably, also no.

It is certainly true that, at the moment, there are differences between Berlin and Warsaw over security policy. Poland has hesitated in accepting Europe's Security and Defence Policy and continues to be full of misgivings. Germany, on the other hand, does not see any rivalry between CESDP and NATO and therefore pleads for a speedy development of the EU's security policy dimension. In contrast to Poland's openly demonstrated support for American missile defence plans, Germany has voiced reservations in principle. Poland's fixation on Ukraine and its concentration on containing Russian influence have for a long time contrasted with Berlin's great, even if not unlimited consideration for Russia. While Berlin for a long time has proceeded with caution to a second NATO enlargement, Poland advocated a speedy next round ever since and even before acceding to NATO membership.

None of the above mentioned points, however, ought to be seen as a serious *threat* to the German-Polish security partnership. On the contrary, we have to note that in almost all of these issues both sides are coming closer to each other. Examples can be found in Poland's more 'pragmatic' approach to the CESDP, the increasingly differentiated German views of missile defence or the starting debate on NATO enlargement in Germany.

Even with regard to Ukraine the contrasts were progressively reduced. As late as summer 2000, the foreign ministries in Paris and Berlin categorically excluded the possibility of Ukraine ever becoming an EU member. Poland, on the other hand, had little understanding for this line of argument. It is true that Berlin did not change its rather negative position concerning a possible perspective for Ukraine becoming an EU member in the far future. But maybe more important than that is the rising attention in Germany concerning the Ukraine, that could lead to discussions about Ukraine's present and future starting between Poland, Germany and France.[47]

Furthermore, it has to be emphasised that despite the differences on some issues, there is a broad consensus on the *basic elements* of the security architecture in Europe between Germany and Poland.

First, both sides consider America's presence in Europe, the maintenance of the transatlantic link and of NATO as its most important institutional epitome, as priorities in the hierarchy of their foreign and security policy objectives.

Second, Poland has – even if not so willingly – distanced itself from its very critical approach to the CESDP and now intends to take an active part in its formation.

Third, Poland has shown its determination to make an important contribution to regional stabilisation, for example, in the Baltic Sea, concerning the Baltic states or Poland's eastern neighbours along the future EU border. This is also an objective of predominant significance for Germany.

Fourth, during the Balkan conflicts Poland has given proof of the fact that it is willing and able to take an active part in trying to solve crises, including, if necessary, military actions at the side of its Alliance partners.

Identifying similarities in the basic security policy objectives of Germany and Poland does not mean diagnosing complete parallelism nor predicting continuing or even increasing tendencies towards mutual rapprochement. To have more than a momentary snapshot portraying simply the current state of security policy objectives and expectations, alternative developments have to be included too. Sketching out such alternatives, two variables in particular must be taken into account: first, German and Polish relations with the US and thus the whole question of transatlantic ties; second, relations with Russia, and thus Polish and German approaches towards other countries of the post-Soviet area. In other words, the complete field of 'Eastern policy'.

With some simplification we could say that these are the two basic determinants (or complexes of determinants) that are responsible for real and potential incongruence in German and Polish security policy objectives. All other determining factors in some sense 'derive' from these basic determinants. Depending on which of the respective orientations is chosen by Germany and Poland, trends towards convergence or divergence will prevail in the long run.

When assessing the further development of Polish-German relations, three scenarios can be posed:

(i)   A scenario of *divergence* and *disparity* would come into existence if Germany turned towards a decided 'Europeanism' while in Poland scepticism against Europe rose significantly. Germany would pursue a more 'Gaullist' policy and orient itself increasingly towards France. In a parallel move, Poland would stand up for Washington even more strongly. As a result, Germany would lose its opportunity to act as mediator between the Atlanticist and the Europeanist camps. Of course, this would not isolate Poland in Europe, but it could become integrated on a lower level. However, seen from today's point of view this scenario is not very likely, if only because of the deeply rooted German Atlanticism.

(ii) The opposite scenario would mean a comprehensive *convergence*. Germany would maintain its course of 'not only but also' trying to harmonise the transatlantic nexus with a heightened European profile. Poland would continue on its road to integration into European structures attempting to act as a medium size power with a flexible 'commitment without enthusiasm' to Europe. It would participate in creating an EU with increased capacity to act and the ability to be an efficient player in security and foreign policy matters. For Germany, Poland would be an equal partner like France and thus become Germany's 'France to the east'.[48] Nevertheless, one should not expect that both sides' views on security will be completely harmonised devoid of any frictions.

(iii) Therefore, a scenario of *decreasing partial incongruence* seems to be the most likely outcome. Its main feature would be a step-by-step process of continuous rapprochement, which, of course, may include inconsistencies and setbacks. Such a development would be based on the ever-broader network of concrete projects of security cooperation in which Germany and Poland are integrated, within multilateral or bilateral frameworks. Diverging interpretations of transatlantic relations would become less and less explosive when the initiation of CESDP is followed by a phase of concrete implementation where questions of practical military character dominate.

If the above scenarios are considered in view of the 11 September 2001 terrorist attacks, the elements of convergence seem to be reinforced. The rather cautious approach concerning Russia's involvement in NATO shows that, in many respects, Germany and Poland now display similar attitudes in dealing with Russia. Some discrepancies as to NATO enlargement have almost evaporated since there is rising support in Berlin for enlargement including the Baltic states. The issue of missile defence, where indeed some disagreement could be observed, has lost explosiveness (at least for the time being) due to the new honeymoon between Russia and the US. With regard to the army review, in Poland as well as in Germany, the establishment of slim, flexible and rapid-reaction armed forces now has become an even greater priority.

All in all, with regard to security policy, the processes induced and catalysed by 11 September 2001 have decreased the potential of friction between Germany and Poland and have created a context conducive to

120

closer security cooperation between the two countries. To use this window of opportunity effectively there is a need for an institutionalised dialogue between the two on security policy and its changing contents that should include governments, parliaments and experts. This could contribute to increasing sensitiveness, on both sides, to locating actual or future discrepancies and trying to mitigate differences.

NOTES

1. See Kai-Olaf Lang, 'Die neuen NATO-Mitglieder und die europäische Sicherheits- und Verteidigungsdimension', *Aktuelle Analysen des BIOst* 52 (1999).
2. Especially France, traditionally the standard bearer of European emancipation from the US, was unhappy with the Polish approach. Terms such as Washington's 'Trojan horse' or America's '51st Federal State' with which French diplomats are said to qualify Poland, illustrate French views of Warsaw.
3. Gerd Föhrenbach, 'Die Außen- und Sicherheitspolitik der Bush-Administration', *Europäische Sicherheit* 7 (2001) pp.11–19.
4. Jügern Chrobog, 'Debatte über die Grundlagen der atlantischen Zivilisation', *Frankfurter Allgemeine Zeitung*, 2 July 2001.
5. Gerhard Schröder, 'Partner für das 21. Jahrhundert', *Frankfurter Allgemeine Zeitung*, 19 Jan. 2001.
6. 'Wie dauerhaft ist die neue transatlantische Solidarität?', *Frankfurter Allgemeine Zeitung*, 29 Oct. 2001.
7. Speech by Chancellor Gerhard Schröder at the Parliamentary Assembly of NATO on the occasion of its 46th annual meeting in Berlin on 21 Nov. 2000 <www.auswaertiges-amt.de>.
8. A paper of the SPD parliamentary caucus says: 'The participation of third states in decision-making processes within the framework of CESDP is not without explosiveness. A direct participation of non-EU member states in internal decision making is impossible.' SPD-Bundestagsfraktion, Die Zukunft der GASP. Sozialdemokratische Perspektiven für die „Gemeinsame Sicherheits- und Außenpolitik', Nov. 2000, p.14.
9. For details see 'Modalities of Consultation and / or Participation for Non-EU European NATO-members', Appendix 1 to the Feira Summit Conclusions.
10. Using the terminology of Franz-Josef Meier in 'Europäische Sicherheits- und Verteidigungsidentität (ESVI) oder Gemeinsame Sicherheits- und Verteidigungspolitik (GESVP)?', ZEI, Discussion Paper 79 (2000) p.49.
11. Reflections of Karsten D. Voigt 'Begründung eines neuen Atlantizismus. Von Partnerschaft zu euroatlantischer Gemeinschaft', *Internationale Politik* 3 (2000) pp.3–10.
12. Hanns W. Maull, 'Germany and the Use of Force: Still a "Civilian Power"?', *Survival* 42/2 (Summer 2000) pp.56–80 quoted in Jolyon Howorth, *European Integration and Defence. The Ultimate Challenge?*, Chaillot Paper 43 (Paris: Institute for Security Studies of the WEU, Paris 2000) p.49.
13. 'Polska ostroznie popiera', *Rzeczpospolita*, 6 Dec. 2001.
14. Rudolf Scharping, 'Die Zukunft Europas mit Russland gestalten', *Süddeutsche Zeitung*, 29 Sept. 2001.
15. See Jaroslaw Drozd, 'Sojusz nadziei. Polsko-niemiecka wspólpraca wojskowa po 1989 roku', Warszawa, 1998.
16. See report submitted by the German Minister of Defence of May 1999 'Die Bundeswehr an der Schwelle zum 21. Jahrhundert' see also 'Neuausrichtung der Bundeswehr - Grobausplanung: Ergebnisse und Entscheidungen'; <www.bundeswehr.de>.
17. See Ryszard Choroszy, 'Leopardyzacje czas zaczoc', *Polska Zbrojna*, 29 May 2001; Tadeusz Wróbel, 'Czolgowy dylemat', *Polska Zbrojna*, 4 Sept. 2001.

18. In this context, it is important to note the choice of Szczecin and a of pre-war German barracks as the corps' headquarters. For example, the then Stettin Mayor Jurczyk had asked for a referendum on the deployment of the corps. See 'Neubeginn auf pommerschem Sand', *Frankfurter Allgemeine Zeitung*, 20 Sept. 1999; 'Gemeinsames Korps in Dienst gestellt', *Berliner Zeitung*, 20 Sept. 1999; Mariusz Urbanczyk, 'NATO nam przyszlo', *Wprost*, 18 Sept. 1999.

19. Delia Meth-Cohn, 'Why do Central Europeans insist on spending so much on the military?', *Business Central Europe* (Oct. 2000).

20. Boleslaw Balcerowicz, 'O pozycje Polski w Sojuszu', in Edward Halizak, Roman Kuzniar, Dariusz Poplawski and Henryk Szlajfer (eds.) *Rocznik strategiczny 1999/2000* (Warszawa 2000) pp.16–23, here p.19.

21. 'Union für Beteiligung an Raketenabwehr', *Frankfurter Allgemeine Zeitung*, 15 March 2001.

22. Karl Lamers, spokesman for foreign affairs of the CDU Bundestag caucus 'Wie beim Zahnarzt', *Frankfurter Allgemeine Zeitung*, 5 Feb. 2001.

23. 'Heftige deutsche Debatte über die NMD', *Neue Zürcher Zeitung*, 2 March 2001.

24. See comments made by Marek Siewiec, President of the National Security Council, and by Defence Minister Komorowski, 'Tarcza dla sojuszników', *Rzeczpospolita*, 23 Feb. 2001; Minister Bronislaw Komorowski, 'dla Rzeczpospolitej', *Rzeczpospolita*, 17 May 2001.

25. Minister Bronislaw Komorowski, 'dla Rzeczpospolitej', *Rzeczpospolita*, 17 May 2001; 'Parasol antyrakietowy nad Polska?', *Rzeczpospolita*, 17 May 2001.

26. The assessment does not seem without reason. The Russian press warned that political support for General Piatas' statements could lead to a 'new phase of cooling in Russian-Polish relations', *Kommersant*, 18 May 2001.

27. Grzegorz Kostrzewa-Zorbas, 'NATO powinno wycofac sie z zobowiazan wobec Rosji', *Rzeczpospolita*, 17–18 Feb. 2001.

28. 'Stanowisko Prezydenta RP w kwestii poszerzenia' in *Rozszerzanie NATO* (Warsaw: Stowarzyszenie Atlantyckic 2000) pp.81–4.

29. Ibid.

30. Statement of Chancellor Schröder, *Financial Times Deutschland*, 15 June 2001.

31. Ex-State Secretary of Defence Lothar Rühl believes that the this opinion is dominating within the German government. Lothar Rühl, 'Pragmatische Osterweiterung der NATO?', *Neue Züricher Zeitung*, 4 Sept. 2001.

32. Janusz Reiter, 'Polska moze współtworzyc wschodni wymiar UE', *Rzeczpospolita*, 18 June 2001.

33. 'In Berlin's view the question of a future EU membership for Ukraine is not under consideration, at the moment.' Ibid.

34. See Auswärtiges Amt, Ministere des Affaires Etrangeres, 'Ein Europa mit dreißig und mehr Mitgliedern. Gemeinsame deutsch-französische Studie' (Joint German-French study Nov. 1998–June 2000) pp.65–6.

35. See Kai-Olaf Lang, 'Polens Beziehungen zu Rußland: Zwischen Argwohn und Zusammenarbeit', *Berichte des Bundesinstituts für ostwissenschaftliche Studien* 31 (2001).

36. Gesamteuropäische Sicherheit unter Einbeziehung Rußlands, speech by the Federal Minister of Defence, Rudolf Scharping, at the Munich Conference for Security Policy on 4 Feb. 2001, <www.bundeswehr.de>.

37. A basic outline of Germany's plans concerning Russia can be found in Chancellor Schröder's article 'Deutsche Russland-Politik – Europäische Ostpolitik', *Zeit*, 5 April 2001; 'Schröder bestimmt seine Russlandpolitik', *Neue Zürcher Zeitung*, 6 April 2001.

38. On this and other problems see Lang (note 33).

39. 'Kryzys przezwyciezony', *Rzeczpospolita*, 31 March – 1 April 2001.

40. Kai-Olaf Lang, 'Ein neues polnisch-russisches Verhältnis?', *SWP Aktuell*, 1 (2002).

41. So Siergiej Karaganov, President of the Council for Foreign and Defence Policy, 'Sosedstvo objazyvaet', *Izviestija*, 16 April 2001.

42. 'Hin zu einer kooperativen Sicherheitspolitik'. Speech given by the coordinator for German-American cooperation in the Foreign Office, Karsten D. Voigt, at the Marshall Center Graduate Symposium, Garmisch-Partenkirchen, 9 May 2001,

43. Boleslaw Balcerowicz, 'O pozycje Polski w Sojuszu' in Haliak *et al.* (note 20) pp.16–23, here p.18.
44. See debate in *Tygodnik Powszechny* on Poland's Eastern Policy.
45. See Centrum Badania Opinii Spoleczne (CBOS) opinion polls 1996–98.
46. Elizbieta Stadtmüller, *Granica leku i nadziei* (Wroclaw: Wydawnictwo Uniwersytetu Wroclawskiego 1999).
47. A public sign of such consultations is the joint Open Letter of the foreign ministers of France, Germany and Poland on the occasion of the Tenth Anniversary of Ukrainian independence, <www.auswaertiges-amt.de>.
48. 'Unser Frankreich im Osten?', *Frankfurter Allgemeine Zeitung*, 16 June 2001.

Poland and Transatlantic Relations in the Twenty-First Century

MARCIN ZABOROWSKI

Nearly four years after becoming a North Atlantic Treaty Organisation (NATO) member Poland is emerging as a participant in transatlantic security. Its involvement in Kosovo and more recently in Afghanistan demonstrated that Poland does not shy away from taking up international responsibilities. Warsaw's lobbying in favour of a second eastern enlargement of NATO and its involvement in promoting civil society in Ukraine, as well as other parts of the former Soviet Union, also demonstrate that Poland sees itself, and acts, as a regional power, and in doing so is supported by the US and other Western allies.[1]

Poland also made itself known as a staunch Atlanticist and a firm supporter of US involvement in Europe. Although Poland's policy towards the EU's defence initiative is likely to become warmer, subject to the development of the EU's eastern policy, it is clear that the Poles see NATO as the main, if not the only, viable security organisation.

This issue shows that Polish security policy is already advanced in acquiring its own profile in the context of transatlantic relations. However, it is clear that, following the events of 11 September 2001, the strategic partnership between Europe and America is going through a process of reformulation. There is no doubt that the outcome of this process will have a strong bearing upon Polish security policy in the forthcoming years. For this reason, it is essential that the preliminary effects of 11 September be addressed in this conclusion.

1. Evolution of Transatlantic Relations after 11 September 2001

The period of time that has elapsed since the dramatic events in America took place may be too short to assess the long-term implications of 11 September 2001 on transatlantic relations. The war on terrorism is far from over and it is likely, as suggested in Bush's 'axis of evil' speech, to escalate further, therefore rendering any predictions as to its ultimate implications appear somewhat speculative.²

Having said that, some general trends resulting from the war on terrorism are already becoming clear and can therefore be incorporated into this analysis. In particular, three developments provide indications as to the future direction of the relationship:

(1) In the crucial stages of its operation in Afghanistan, America preferred to act unilaterally, allowing only for the limited involvement of other forces and relying on the logistical support from countries outside the core of the transatlantic alliance, such as Pakistan, Uzbekistan and Russia. Despite numerous offers from various European NATO members, until the Taliban regime crumbled in December 2001 the only non-American units permitted by the US to participate in combat missions on the ground in Afghanistan were British SAS and a handful of French and Australian special forces.³

On the other hand, it appears that while the US remained reluctant about involving Europeans in actual combat it expected them to play to crucial role in providing civil order and aid for the reconstruction of Afghanistan.⁴

(2) Despite NATO invoking Article 5 in response to the terrorist attack on America, so far little use has been made of either NATO military assets or its political institutions, which did not serve as the primary forum for consultation between the US and Europeans. Consequently, the relevance of NATO as an organisation of collective defence is increasingly questioned.

(3) The crisis saw the emergence of a European 'directorate' – a group of the three biggest (in military terms) EU member states: Britain, France and Germany, who chose to consult their national responses to the events in Afghanistan, as well as to pursue some degree of coordination in the framework of the EU. This was received with some suspicion and annoyance by other European states. On one hand, it is clear that the EU needs to develop its own defence and that this can be done only if the 'big three' push it ahead. On the other hand, the emergence of a Franco-British-German directorate raised fears of marginalisation among the smaller (i.e. Benelux) or less-influential (i.e. Italy, Spain) EU member states.⁵

Overall, the events of 11 September have demonstrated that the transatlantic alliance is, in fact, looser and more diverse than its popular image in Poland would suggest. This is not to say that the relationship is actually losing its relevance. In many respects the contrary could be argued. For example, it is an unquestionable fact that, in reaction to the terrorist attacks in the US, the world saw the greatest expression of Europe's solidarity with America since the end of the Cold War. Yet, it is also clear from the three points outlined above that the transatlantic alliance will not return to what it used to be and that it will continue to evolve.

Adrian Hyde-Price presented four scenarios for the future development of the transatlantic relationship; 'reborn partnership', 'divorce', 'continental drift' and 'partial rapprochement'. While 'divorce' represents an end to the relationship and 'continental drift' means sliding towards 'divorce', the other two scenarios, 'reborn partnership' and 'partial rapprochement' suggest an improvement in the relationship, in the first instance more considerable than in the second. Post-11 September, developments indicate that two of these scenarios 'partial rapprochement' or 'continental drift' are most likely to replace the earlier condition of US-European relations.

The question may arise at this point as to what kind of evolution of transatlantic security is likely to be endorsed by Poland. As demonstrated here, despite some of its policy contradictions, Poland appears firmly committed to the strengthening of security links between Europe and the US, a policy which in fact became a new-found dogma in Polish security thinking. It is unlikely that Warsaw's commitment to the transatlantic relationship would be challenged domestically in the foreseeable future, irrespective of who is in government. The current coalition of ex-communist Social Democrats (SLD) and the Peasant Party (PSL) appears to be continuing with the foreign policy of its Solidarity-led predecessor, including its political Atlanticism.

It is clear therefore that if the transatlantic relationship has to change (and Warsaw would prefer that it does not) Poland would be most likely to work towards its 're-birth' or at least 'partial rapprochement'. While 'continental drift' would be perceived by Warsaw as undesirable, a 'divorce' would be seen as nothing short of a catastrophe. A realisation of any of the pessimistic scenarios would mean for Poland exposure to regional instability, which cost the country so dearly in the past.

Leaving aside for a moment the grand question of whether transatlantic relations will evolve towards 'continental drift' or 'partial rapprochement', it is clear that the implications of 11 September demonstrated the increasing 'nationalisation' of security policies on both sides of the Atlantic. Both the Americans and Europeans, in particular the British, German and French, chose to ignore existing international institutions, NATO in the first and the EU in the second instance, and responded in a way that underlined the traditional role of nation-states as primary security providers.[6]

Consequently, so far the crisis has seen a weakening of the defensive roles of international institutions and the emergence of small coalitions based on the three following kinds of interest reciprocity:

(i)   The existence of a long-term close military relationship – US with Britain and to a much lesser extent with France and Australia.

(ii) Specific war theatre-related issue – US with Pakistan and Uzbekistan

(iii) Strategic (though potentially temporary) concord of regional interests – US with Russia.[7]

These developments demonstrate that, when vital security issues are involved, nation-states are anything but redundant. This is also reflected in this publication. Although its structure was decided many months before 11 September, the assumption behind the project was that national case studies should form the core of our investigations. The findings of this thematic issue seem to confirm that we were not mistaken in assuming that Poland's role in transatlantic security is to be first and foremost determined through its relations with other European states and America.

2. Poland and its Partners in the Transatlantic Partnership

America

It was argued here that Poland located itself at the Atlanticist end of the US-European debate. Yet, it is a particular kind of Atlanticism – one that remains rather stuck to the past as demonstrated in Warsaw's continuing stress on NATO's defensive role and its ambivalent attitude towards building more mobile armed forces. As seen in the article by David Dunn, these 'old-fashioned' elements of Poland's security doctrine failed to impress Warsaw's new cherished partner – the US. It is likely, following the events of 11 September, that Washington's dissatisfaction with Warsaw will only increase, should the latter continue to define its security in a predominantly defensive way.

However, despite the existence of these discrepancies in US and Polish defence strategies, there is a far-reaching affinity of views, perspectives and policies between Warsaw and Washington, which is likely to continue in the foreseeable future. Certainly, Washington's relations with Warsaw are more intimate then those with other ex-communist states, including the other new NATO members – Hungary and the Czech Republic. In fact, it is fair to say that Washington 'gets on better' with Warsaw than with many long-standing partners in the transatlantic alliance. The US request for Poland's military contribution to the operation in Afghanistan and Warsaw's immediate and positive response, is just one indication of how close this relationship is.[8]

On the other hand, it is important to note that if the current status of the relationship is to endure, the US must resist the temptation to treat Poland as one of its client states. Although Poland's political Atlanticism is unquestionable, it is not certain that it will extend to economic issues, as the US seems to suggest should be the case. The testing case here will be the outcome of the Polish jet fighter tender, which is marked by fierce competition between American F-16s, French Mirages and Swedish Gripens. After being snubbed by the Czechs and Hungarians, both of which chose Gripens, Americans are insisting that Poland's choice should not be based on economic but rather strategic grounds.[9]

It is difficult not see a thinly disguised element of political blackmailing in Washington's argument on the jet fighter issue, with a consequence of this being, for the first time since the collapse of communism, an emerging public debate in Poland about the costs and desirability of Atlanticism.[10]

In addition, with the events of 11 September, changes occurred in American foreign policy that are less conducive with Poland's priorities. Two developments in particular are of significance in this context: American unilateralism, and with it a weakening of NATO, and second an emergence of a new partnership between the US and Russia. Just as American unilateralism directly contradicts Poland's objective to maintain strong transatlantic ties and the US's engagement in Europe, the pro-Russian shift in Washington threatens to dilute American support for the Westernisation of Ukraine and the rest of the former Soviet Union.

Warsaw is also anxious about an apparent weakening of NATO as seen in the Alliance's low profile in the operation in Afghanistan.

Germany, France and Britain

At the initial stages of designing this project it was assumed that the study would confirm whether, in its behaviour, Poland resembles one of the larger European states: Germany, Britain or France. However, no such conclusions proved possible; instead, it appears that Poland brings into the transatlantic relationship a new and original quality that does not quite seem to have a precedence. Interestingly, when compared with its West European partners, it seems that Poland combines some of the most outstanding hallmarks of their security policies, yet, in doing so it represents a distinctive model itself.

As seen in the report by Silke Pottebohm, Poland shares with Britain its political Atlanticism, but it differs considerably in its military capability and organisation of its force structure.

With Germany, Poland shares the practice of universal male conscription as well as its low level of defence spending and within it a low proportion being spent on research and development. On the other hand, as seen in the article by Kai-Olaf Lang, Germany has remained ambivalent about taking upon itself a greater international role – an issue that Poland has never had any hesitations about.

As seen in Vanda Knowles's article, there are striking similarities in France's and Poland's deep attachments to their national identities and their conviction that their countries are destined to play a considerable international role. Yet, at the same time, France and Poland remain at opposing ends of the transatlantic debate as apparent in their diametrically divergent policies towards the EU's defence initiatives.

Clearly, with some of the European states dealt with here Poland has had closer security relations than with others. As argued in the article by Lang, Poland's relations with Germany appear particularly intimate. Not only was Germany a key promoter of Poland's NATO membership, but it also worked hard towards integrating Poland's armed forces with their Western counterparts through joint exercises and the training of Polish officers at the Bundeswehr universities.[11]

Furthermore, the joint German-Polish-Danish corps remains the only multinational force in existence that was formed across the former East–West divide. It is difficult to see why this already well-developed cooperation would not flourish further when Poland joins the EU.

The report by Pottebohm on Poland's security relations with Britain paints the picture of a friendly yet somehow detached relationship. While, on one hand, Britain and Poland are connected by ideological affinity based on wartime camaraderie and more recently on their political atlanticism, on the other hand, they remain detached both in a geographical and a cultural sense. Consequently, it can be expected that for Britain Poland can continue to be perceived as its major partner in Central and Eastern Europe, but the relationship is unlikely to become as intensive as the one between Poland and Germany.

As seen in the article by Vanda Knowles, Poland's relations with France were historically intimate and very good. Both countries have had shared experiences (e.g., Polish participation in Napoleon's army) and common interests, including struggles against belligerent Prussia and then Germany. The Polish intelligentsia developed strong Francophile tendencies during the nineteenth and most of the twentieth century and, as argued by Knowles, even today the French are among the most favoured nations in Poland. During the most recent era, Paris gained Warsaw's gratitude for its support for the Polish position during the Oder/Neisse border dispute.[12]

However, despite this overwhelmingly positive record of past relations, Polish-French cooperation experienced growing divergences from the end of the Cold War. Knowles argues that two factors contributed to this development: first the French disinterest in Central and Eastern Europe and second Poland's overt Atlanticism and pro-Americanism, which goes against the grain of French political culture. The second of these elements meant that, despite their historical amity, as far as transatlantic security is concerned, Poland and France find each other at opposing sides of debates.

Overall the country-focused case studies indicate that outside America, it is probably Germany with which Poland's security relations are most likely to develop in the most progressive manner. Not only have Polish-German relations advanced considerably since the end of the Cold War, in the defence field more so than anywhere else, but also there are some similarities between Poland's current and West Germany's former security positions as the bordering states of the alliance. It is therefore unsurprising that the Poles find more sympathy for their specific security concerns in Berlin than anywhere else in NATO.

As seen in the individual parts of this issue, Poland's ability to become a valuable partner in NATO and establish genuine partnership with America, Germany, France, UK, or any other member state, will depend on Warsaw's capacity to find its own niche – a specific role for itself in the Alliance and make its contribution indispensable. As argued by Kerry Longhurst, the area where Poland's contribution appears most obvious is in the East, and in particular the European parts of the former Soviet Union.

3. Poland's contribution to the Alliance – the East

As argued by Kerry Longhurst a view emanating from Brussels is that Poland is expected to play a vital role in developing NATO's and the EU's policy vis-à-vis the former Soviet Union. It is usually argued in this context that due to its geographical location, its history and linguistic kinship, Poland is ideally located to act as a transmitter of reforms or as a bridge between East and West.

However, a note of caution is needed here. Although it is true that in the past Poland was strongly involved in the East, as seen in the report by Roman Wolczuk, the history of this engagement has been anything but short of controversy. From the early seventeenth century onwards, the Polish-Lithuanian commonwealth was in constant conflict with the Russian empire over the division of influence in the lands 'in-between' (Ukraine and Belarus), which ended in the defeat and collapse of the Polish-Lithuanian state at the end of the eighteenth century.

Although subsequently Poland was wiped off the political maps of Europe (until 1918) its gentry retained a dominant economic position in Ukraine, Belarus and Lithuania, which in the age of emerging national awareness of these nations led to the emergence of anti-Polish sentiments in the East.

The post-1918 Second Polish Republic was a highly heterogeneous entity with its eastern provinces being heavily populated by Ukrainians, Lithuanians and Belorussians, all of whom were subjected to the policy of forced assimilation leading to the further growth of anti-polonism among these nations.

The anti-Polish traits of eastern Slavic and Lithuanian national movements were still present after the end of the Cold War, as apparent in the dispute over the status of the Polish minority in Lithuania or the discussion over the renovation of the Polish cemetery in Lviv in present day Ukraine.[13]

It is therefore clear that when acting in the East, Poland must be cautious not to tread on anybody's toes and in particular not to give an impression that it is projecting its own self-interest under the umbrella of NATO and the EU. It appears that after the initial post-Cold War period, which was marked by some nationalistic overtures apparent on both sides, Warsaw has been on track in establishing a genuine partnership with Lithuania and Ukraine. Most importantly, in both cases Warsaw served as an advocate of these states' closer ties with the West. For example, Poland became an outspoken supporter of Lithuania's NATO membership.[14]

As argued by Wolczuk, Warsaw also supported Ukraine's closer ties with the EU and its inclusion in various Central European fora and institutions, such as the Central European Initiative, Central European Free Trade Area (CEFTA) and the regular meetings of Central European Presidents.[15]

However, although Poland's eastern policy has been relatively successful in Lithuania and Ukraine, the same is not true for Russia and Belarus. As far as Belarus is concerned the dictatorial rule of the country's eccentric president Lukashenko and his evident nostalgia for the Soviet Union served as a major barrier to Warsaw playing an active role in this country. Yet, the same justification cannot be given to explain why since the end of the Cold War Polish-Russian relations have suffered. To be sure, Warsaw is not solely responsible for the current ambivalence in its relations with Moscow.

In the eyes of Poles and other Central Europeans, Russia has been painfully slow in coming to terms with the past and acknowledging its historical wrongdoing towards the nations it subjected to its communist rule. Subsequently, and not unrelated with the former, Russia's opposition to NATO enlargement came to be perceived in Poland as a continuation of Moscow's imperial ambitions and an attempt to retain some leverage over security arrangements in Central and Eastern Europe.

Finally, Russia's constant meddling in the internal affairs of, what it described as, its 'near abroad' and particularly in Belarus, Ukraine and Moldova were often seen in Warsaw as further proof of enduring Russian ambitions in Eastern Europe.

All these factors affected the Polish elite's ability to put aside historical arguments and start perceiving Russia as a potential partner rather than an un-reconstructed bully and a threat. It is in this context that Warsaw's occasional over-sensitivity and clumsiness in relations with Moscow needs to be seen. Probably, the most spectacular manifestation of this historically-laden approach was declaring as *personae non grate* and asking to leave the country the nine Russian diplomats who were accused of spying in January 2000.[16] Regardless of whether the Russian diplomats were spying or not (all evidence suggests that they were) it was most unusual of the host state to publicise this kind of diplomatic incident rather than to sort it out quietly. This clearly did not improve already sensitive relations.

What is, however, important here is the fact that this continuing lack of trust in Polish-Russian relations has had a significant impact on Polish security and defence strategy, which, as argued earlier, remains focused on territorial defence. Poland's rather conservative defence policy has been criticised in NATO, as well as the EU and by the US. It therefore appears that the condition of Poland's relations with Russia is of direct importance for the organisation of its security (including the practice of conscription) and, as a consequence, for Poland's position in transatlantic relations.

The current balance of Warsaw's eastern policy remains therefore still rather mixed.

It is probably fair to say that despite existing historical difficulties and sensitivities, Warsaw fulfilled the expectations placed upon it by its Western partners with regard to Lithuania and Ukraine.

The record of its relations with Moscow is less impressive. Although no major problem emerged in the post-Cold War period, relations did not develop beyond a rather cool coexistence. As argued above, Warsaw can hardly be blamed alone for this state of affairs, but it is also true that there is an urgent need to re-examine the perception of Russia in Poland as a potential aggressor. Not only is such a perception increasingly received as anachronistic in the West, particularly in the aftermath of 11 September, but it also affects Poland's ability to embark on a comprehensive review of its security and defence policies.

Indeed, it seems that Warsaw is increasingly recognising that its importance and respect in the West are directly linked to its relations with the East and Russia in particular. It is, perhaps, in this context that following the events of 11 September, Warsaw intensified its efforts to improve relations with Moscow, a task that was helped by a pro-Western shift in Russian foreign policy.

It is not insignificant here that Polish-Russian relations were discussed during the Polish Prime Minister, Leszek Miller's, visit to Washington in January 2002.[17] The subsequent visit of the Russian President Putin in Warsaw demonstrated that Russian attitudes towards Poland are changing for the better.[18] All of this indicates that Poland and Russia seem to be approaching a much-delayed breakthrough in their relations. However, there is no room for complacency here – there is no doubt that Poland's eastern policy has to develop further if it is really to become Warsaw's major contribution to the transatlantic alliance in the twenty-first century.

4. Transatlantic Relations and Polish Security and Defence Policy in the Twenty-First Century

Although it is not certain whether in the twenty-first century the transatlantic alliance will experience 'rebirth', 'drift' or 'partial rapprochement', some aspects of its future evolution are becoming apparent. For example, it is almost inevitable that the scope of the alliance will continue to grow in the eastwards direction by means of a twofold and most probably simultaneous development. On one hand, NATO will continue to expand its membership, the next round of enlargement was announced at the November 2002 summit in Prague. On the other hand, Russia and to a lesser extent Ukraine, while formally non-members, are increasingly involved in NATO's decision-making process.

This broadening of the scope of the transatlantic alliance will come hand in hand with the redefinition of its role. Although this process has been taking place since the end of the Cold War, it has become ever more urgent since 11 September 2001. For one thing, since the terrorist attacks on America it is even clearer that the age of mass armies and territorial defence is well and truly over. For contemporary security challenges greater emphasis needs to be placed upon intelligence and, as far as the defence sector is concerned, on the further development of mobile, smaller and highly trained professional forces.

The question that emerges here is whether Poland is prepared to face up to these contemporary and future developments in transatlantic security. Clearly, one would have imagined that with Warsaw's apparent ambition to play an important role in transatlantic relations, Poland would join the vanguard of reform-minded countries and move swiftly towards the modernisation of its security agenda and capabilities. Though it is true that some steps have been taken in this direction, the six-year reform plan was approved by the former parliament, this has not been seen as sufficient by Poland's western neighbours as well as by NATO and the EU. Moreover, it seems that the already moderate reform will become a victim of the austerity plan of the new SLD-PSL government.[19]

Yet it is clear that if the transatlantic link is to survive and, as argued here, its further maintenance is in Poland's national interest, European member states have to improve their contribution to the security of the Euro-Atlantic area. This call applies to Poland, and other new members of the Alliance, in no smaller part than to the older ones.

Whereas Poland has been successful overall in developing its own 'profile' within NATO the extent of its contribution to the Alliance remains questionable. The evidence gathered in this report suggests that further steps have to be taken in order for Poland to join the core of Europe's 'security providers', and to see its transatlantic ambitions fulfilled. In particular, the four following recommendations seem most apparent:

1. Defence spending must be maintained at the level of least 2 per cent of gross domestic product and it must be better used. Most crucially, fewer resources should be spent on the maintenance of the existing vast and often non-defence related infrastructure whilst more money should be directed towards equipment modernisation as well as research.
2. Force structure should be considerably reformed. There should be fewer territorial defence units and more rapid reaction forces. Conscription should be abolished and the conscript army should be replaced by a smaller, more mobile and better trained all volunteer force.
3. There is an urgent need to develop an independent research community specialising in defence and security issues, which would aid defence and foreign ministries.

4. On the policy level it seems apparent that while Warsaw's policy towards Ukraine and Lithuania has worked towards strengthening Poland's international position, the same has not been yet the case with Polish-Russian relations. Although Warsaw should continue rejecting Moscow's policy of achieving some kind of special status in European security, there is an urgent need for Warsaw to establish more cooperative relations with Russia and move beyond historically-determined perceptions.

This issue argue that in all of the policy areas mentioned above, Poland is already moving along the lines aimed at strengthening its contribution to the Alliance. However, as was also maintained financial, cultural and historical constraints continue to hinder the modernisation process. There is no doubt that a great deal has already been achieved to overcome existing constraints, however, much more remains to be done if Poland is to meet its own political ambitions and become a meaningful actor in transatlantic relations.

NOTES

1. See Warsaw speech by George W. Bush, 15 June 2001; Przemowienie Prezydenta W. Busha w Bibliotece Uniwersytetu Warszawskiego, *Gazeta Wyborcza*, 15 June 2001.
2. 'George W. Bush and the axis of evil', *The Economist*, 2 Feb. 2002.
3. Colin Powell at the OSCE News Conference in Romania, 4 Dec. 2001, BBC News report
4. 'America and Europe – who needs whom?' *The Economist*, 9 March 2002.
5. 'Guess who wasn't coming to dinner?' *The Economist*, 10 Nov. 2001.
6. On the question of 'nationalisation' of European security and defence policy see: 'Power to the capitals', *Financial Times*, 15 Oct. 2001.
7. 'Suddenly, such good neighbours', *The Economist*, 10 Nov. 2001
8. 'Poland to contribute Specialised Troops to Help Afghan Mission', *NATO Enlargement Daily Brief*, 6 Dec. 2001.
9. 'Amerykanie naciskaja w sprawie F-16', *Rzeczpospolita*, 12 Jan. 2001.
10. 'Sto slow', *Trybuna*, 11 Jan. 2001
11. V. Handl, K. Longhurst, M. Zaborowski , 'Germany's Security Policy Towards East Central Europe', *Perspectives – The Central European Review of International Affairs* 14 (Summer 2000) pp.54–71.
12. Unpublished PhD thesis by M. Zaborowski, *The Europeanisation of Polish-German Relations*, Institute for German Studies at the University of Birmingham (2001) pp.120–6.
13. See contribution to this issue by Roman Wolczuk.
14. For example see a speech by President Kwasniewski given during George W. Bush's visit in Warsaw: 'Wystapienie prezydenta Aleksandra Kwasniewskiego', *Rzeczpospolita*, 16 June 2001.
15. Also see 'Poland:Eastern Relations', *Oxford Analytica-East Europe Daily Brief*, 8 Aug. 2000.
16. 'Dyplomaci rosyjscy szpiegami', *Rzeczpospolita*, 21 Jan. 2001.
17. 'Miller u Busha', *Trybuna*, 12 Jan. 2002.
18. 'Gesty rosyjskiego prezydenta', *Rzeczpospolita*, 17 Jan. 2001. 'Dobra atmosfera, malo konkretow', *Rzeczpospolita*, 18 Jan. 2001.
19. 'Mniej pieniedzy na wojsko', *Rzeczpospolita*, 26 Oct. 2001.

Poland and Britain: The Future of an Atlanticist Partnership in Europe

SILKE POTTEBOHM

Poland is viewed by the United Kingdom as an ally dating back to World War II; a new member of NATO and a future member of the EU, and Britain is looking to develop its relationship with Poland in terms of close cooperation and partnership building. Particularly in the field of security, Poland is an important ally because of its military weight and its geostrategic significance. Britain regards Poland not only as an important addition to both organisations, but also as a valuable ally within the alliance and the union.

The future of the relationship between Britain and Poland in the context of transatlantic relations, however, raises various questions. While both countries agree on the political aspects of transatlantic relations, there are differences over the importance of Article 5 of the North Atlantic Treaty and the cooperation between NATO and Russia. Britain also has sceptical views about Polish military capabilities. Poland, on the other hand, is not completely at ease with the fast development of a Common Security and Defence Policy of the European Union. These issues and their importance for British-Polish relations will be addressed in the following report.[1]

There is a lack of informed opinion about Poland among British defence policy-makers. Those people who do think about Poland's position are generally experts who are involved and in contact with the Polish side in negotiations and diplomatic interactions. Polish security issues are not a matter of public debate in Britain and there is no measurable or informed opinion about Polish security issues.

A good overall perception of Polish security policy, which is underlined with a positive attitude towards the country, was found among the experts and policy-makers interviewed for this report, but there is a lack of knowledge about specific issues of Polish security policy.

Polish Military Capabilities

Poland's NATO membership is seen, overall, as beneficial in terms of extending the zone of security. There are, however, concerns and expectations. In terms of Poland's military performance as a new member of NATO, British experts have described the Polish efforts in the process of joining the alliance as over ambitious, especially in relation to the performance of other members. Among the established members of NATO there was, at the same time, an over optimism and a slightly unrealistic attitude towards the speed at which those new members could be absorbed into the Alliance.

British experts stress the value of Poland's strong military tradition, its strategic position and links with other eastern European countries. The British view of Polish security policy starts with the perception that Poland's national security and defence policy is a result of its history. From this follows Poland's focus on the fact that it is a newly liberated country with a big neighbour in the east that is not fully trusted. Overall the basic pattern of military reform and the security doctrine of Poland are considered to be moving in the right direction.

From a political point of view, Poland's security policy is aligned with the British position. British experts did, however, express concerns about certain aspects of military reform in Poland. On a theoretical level of reform, Poland has been portrayed as being far ahead of the others. Poland is perceived to comprehend that NATO is developing into a more political alliance.

Whenever critical views on Poland's performance have been formulated, there has been, at the same time, an acknowledgement of the fact that Poland has only been out of the Warsaw Pact since the end of the Cold War and joined NATO only in March 1999. Polish armed forces as they exist have been built by a different system with a different purpose and the transformation process is expected to require a long time. Polish performance in NATO is seen critically in some aspects, but positively overall.

In general there was no immediate expectations on Poland to speed up reforms, because there was no threat that would dictate a more rapid pace. Nevertheless, there was a clear expectation in Britain that the Polish contribution towards NATO security should grow in line with future economic performance. This has changed in the light of the events of 11 September 2001, which is why the British Secretary of State for Defence commissioned a further chapter for the Strategic Defence Review. This additional chapter of the Strategic Defence Review is looking at the impact of the attacks on 11 September on British defence posture and capabilities.[2]

Article 5

In the context of military reform there is also the question of changing hardware and the need to make it fully interoperable within NATO to allow greater participation in NATO missions. British experts stress the importance of Poland rebuilding its army by taking into account the changes in today's security environment, in order to prepare for tasks ranging from peacekeeping to peace enforcement. Instead of focusing solely on tasks arising out of Article 5 of the North Atlantic Treaty, Poland should also develop military capacity that would enable the country to participate in missions related to the Petersberg tasks.[3] The keywords in this context are readiness and deployability.[4]

This debate is becoming increasingly important to discussions on the future of NATO. After the terrorist attacks on America, the alliance evoked Article 5 of the Washington Treaty, although, this was not followed by a NATO military operation. The US is looking to its European partners for support in providing humanitarian help and in dealing with the aftermath of the military attacks on Afghanistan. The tasks arising here are peacekeeping and state building. One aspect of strengthening the political and diplomatic dimension of NATO is the growing importance of tasks relating to peacekeeping and state building. NATO member states that want to retain their influence within the alliance must adjust their security policy according to these developments.

Common European Security and Defence Policy (CESDP)

The terrorists' attacks on the US also triggered a new urgency to develop a military capacity that would underline the Common European Security and Defence Policy (CESDP). Britain, together with other member states, has stressed the importance of reaching the target of a European defence capability. In general, London understands Poland's concerns about territorial defence, but also expects Poland to improve its ability to participate in peacekeeping operations and to contribute towards the European Rapid Reaction Force thereby enhancing European capabilities.

Although the development of CESDP has been pursued with the support of Britain, France and Germany, it can be seen as a project close to the heart of Britain's Labour administration. The Prime Minister Tony Blair has chosen a policy area that allows him to exert political control at home and at the same time exercise leadership in the European policy arena.

British policy-makers have expressed expectations on the Polish contribution to European Security and Defence up to now. Within NATO, where the British presence is strong, there is some element of dissatisfaction about the Polish contribution. Britain wants Poland to step up its actions and to become a net contributor to common defence: both in NATO and by making a new quality of contribution to European defence. Of all the EU applicant states, Poland has the biggest land force, apart from Turkey. By joining the EU it would be expected to play a major role and as it is mainly Britain and France who provide capabilities for the European Rapid Reaction Force the British would welcome this. As Polish assets are already integrated in the NATO command structure, an integration of the Polish army into the European Rapid Reaction Force capabilities would be seen to strengthen the European Security and Defence Identity within NATO. In conclusion it can be said that Poland, as it is not a member of the EU, is not yet seen to be an actor in CESDP.

Poland and its Eastern Neighbours

One of the major focal points of Poland's NATO membership is the country's relations with its neighbours in Eastern Europe. Relations between Poland and its neighbours are perceived to be rapidly improving.

First, Poland's NATO membership stabilises the region and prepares an environment in which Poland can create and cultivate its relations with eastern neighbours, such as the Ukraine, Russia and Belarus.[5]

Second, Poland's geostrategic position, its past and its links with several sensitive countries are important to NATO. The expertise of the Polish government, based on historic links and shared borders, is invaluable for the alliance.

Third, Poland is seen as a role model for economic and military reform in former communist countries. Poland, as the largest and wealthiest country to join the alliance, had to make its membership a success in order to garner support for further NATO enlargement, both within existing members, and also among future applicant states. This is one reason for the special importance of the first round of NATO enlargement. This argument is also valid for the forthcoming enlargement of the European Union.

The North Atlantic Alliance is facing key decisions at its November 2002 summit in Prague. The summit will outline the military and political future of the alliance by deciding on new additions to the alliance and on the possibility of strengthening its cooperation with Russia in certain policy areas. Britain and Poland face differences over the enlargement of the alliance and closer collaboration between NATO and Russia.

An important consideration for Britain's position on further NATO enlargement is the alliance's experience of integrating Poland, Hungary and the Czech Republic. Overall, British policy-makers do not view the Czech Republic and the Hungary's contribution towards the alliance as very positive. The main point of criticism is the lack of contribution towards the security dimension of the alliance. This could be an important factor in the debate about further NATO enlargement.

There is no official British government position on the integration of the Baltic States into NATO, but some British policy-makers and senior civil servants have expressed their concerns by pointing out that it would be very difficult for NATO to extend its Article 5 guarantee to the Baltic States. The British perspective favours cooperation in this region. A fast integration of the Baltic States into NATO could be seen as a provocative act by Moscow within Russian-NATO relations.

There is a view, however, that despite this America favours the integration of Lithuania, Estonia and Latvia into NATO, due to the influence of powerful ethnic pressure groups in the US. By the time of the Prague NATO summit in 2002 there might be a drive in favour of NATO membership for Lithuania, which Britain will not be able to resist. There is also a British awareness that Poland would favour integrating the Baltic States into NATO.

The terrorist attacks on the US, and its retaliation, have added further momentum to the question of NATO enlargement. Prompted by the handling of military action against Afghanistan, the question of the future of NATO and the balance between NATO's military and political missions were raised. The military dimension of NATO has always coexisted with a political dimension, though in future the latter is likely to gain even more weight in determining the structure and activities of the alliance.[6]

In Britain a debate has begun about the prospect of enhancing the political dimension of NATO, which in the light of the global alliance against terrorism would also mean reviewing possible future applicant states and building strong links with former enemies.[7] Nevertheless, it can be concluded that the British position on NATO enlargement is still dominated by hesitant caution.

British experts seem less aware of Polish-Russian relations, which are described as historically not very good and hawkish. Some British policy-makers have linked Poland's concern over national defence and the high importance of NATO's Article 5 for the country to unsolved Russian-Polish questions. However, there was a perception among the interviewees that relations improved after Poland joined NATO. This is described as a positive political benefit of NATO membership. Poland is seen as an excellent interpreter of the Russian scene and in this respect can be very useful for improved relations between NATO and Russia.

The events of 11 September 2001 and the subsequent campaign against terrorism have triggered a debate over the closer involvement of Russia in NATO affairs. In accordance with NATO Secretary-General, Lord Robertson, Prime Minister Tony Blair has suggested a revision of the existing NATO-Russia Permanent Council. The British proposal aims to involve Russia much more closely and on a more practical level in NATO affairs. NATO-Russian co-operation should include '... security co-operation in the fight against terrorism, countering proliferation of weapons of mass destruction, peace support operations and dealing with new threats'.[8]

However the British outline for an enhanced structure of opportunities for joint action by a NATO in effect of 20 members, has not only met opposition from the US National Security Council and the Pentagon, but also from European NATO members. Poland, Hungary and the Czech Republic in particular, felt that a Russian veto over decisions in the alliance would be a step too far. The British proposal was not discussed in advance with NATO partners. When Britain distributed the proposal, it caused concern among NATO partners and prompted Warsaw to asked London for clarification.

The British intention was to reward Russia for supporting the campaign against terrorism with closer integration into NATO. Poland, however, together with other former Warsaw Pact countries, which are now NATO members or a applying to join the alliance, have voiced their opposition to a Russia-North Atlantic Council in which Russia would have a right of veto. Whilst countries like Poland are very sensitive about closer Russian-NATO cooperation, Britain has shown a lack of understanding, by going public with its proposals without considering the Warsaw Pact legacy of the new NATO members.

Both issues, NATO enlargement and the alliance's future relations with Russia, bear the potential for causing conflicts within British-Polish relations and require consideration from both sides, especially in the context of alliance building.

Conclusion

In terms of relationship-building between Britain and Poland a distinction has to be made between the arena of the European Union and the platform of the Transatlantic Alliance. It remains to be seen if and how EU membership will change Poland's loyalties. After joining the EU, Poland could become more European. On the other hand, Poland as a member of the EU could make the European Union's security policy more Atlanticist. On the whole, it is anticipated that Poland will become a strong British ally in the EU in pursing a transatlantic agenda within the Union. As a senior defence analyst summed it up: 'Britain needs all the allies in the EU it can get, because of its somewhat peculiar position.'[9]

Within NATO there already exists a special relationship between Poland and the US. British-Polish partnership building will need to take into account the special relationships that both countries have already built and supported for a long time. As the US is the partner for both countries' special relationships, this should serve as common ground. Poland and the UK have a long history of partnership and Poland is perceived as a NATO member that shares British positions and attitudes. Both countries share Western values and are good Atlanticists. But there are still possible areas of conflict.

Polish forces are still seen to carry a certain legacy of under investment and poor organisation from Warsaw Pact days. There is a clear perception that Poland is serious in wanting to make improvements in order to contribute to NATO, but also awareness that this process will take longer than expected. Another possible area of conflict is the emphasis on NATO's Article 5 guarantee, and in particular, the importance of territorial defence in Polish security policy. By the time Poland joins the EU, British policy-makers expect Poland to be able to make a real contribution to the CESDP and to tasks arising from new security challenges.

A possible second area of conflict could be further NATO enlargement. Britain does not oppose further enlargement, but desires a process of cooperation for the time being, which would lead towards further enlargement in the more distant future. Poland, on the other hand, seems to support a faster process. On this matter, the Polish position seems to be closer to US thinking.

A similar conclusion can be reached in relation to Tony Blair's plans for closer security cooperation between NATO and Russia. British proposals for a Russia-North Atlantic Council, including a Russian veto, were watered down under pressure from the US and the former Warsaw Pact NATO members. It will also be important to see which positions both countries will develop on missile defence and where British and Polish differences or similarities on this question are.

The development of the CESDP of the EU, on the other hand, opens up common ground between the two countries. Britain and Poland fear that if an isolationist movement within the European Union were to gain control, the US could turn away from Europe. For this reason they will try to steer CESDP away from an anti-American direction. Furthermore, both countries share the feeling that Russia is of prime concern for the future of European security for a variety of reasons.

The emerging strains of the development of CESDP and missile defence on the alliance are also strains for Poland, placing the country in a position between the EU and NATO. British policy-makers are concerned that Poland must not be seen to diminish NATO's ability to participate in European security policy. The British view about this state of affairs is that the security guarantee that emanates from NATO is an American compound as well a European one. For Poland, being a member of NATO is being an ally of the US and if there had to be a choice, there would be a clear preference for the US over European neighbours in defence terms. In a potential conflict within the alliance, in which a choice had to be made between the US and Europe, Poland is expected to support the US position and in this sense it is very similar to Britain.

NOTES

1. This report is based largely on extensive confidential interviews with defence policy decision-makers and parliamentarians in the UK.
2. Geoff Hoon, Secretary of State for Defence, '11 September – A new chapter for the Strategic Defence Review'. Speech at King's College, London, 5 Dec. 2001.
3. The Petersberg Tasks were based on the 1992 'Petersberg declaration' of the WEU Council of Ministers and are incorporated in article 17-2 of the Amsterdam Treaty of the European Union committing all member states of the EU. The Petersberg Tasks include humanitarian intervention and evacuation operations; peacekeeping; the use of combat forces in crisis management, including peacemaking. These tasks require military action, but do not relate to national security and defence in a traditional context.
4. Confidential interviews in London in summer 2001.
5. Ibid.
6. Charles Grant 'Does this war show that NATO no longer has a serious military role?' *Independent*, 16 Oct. 2001, p.11.
7. Richard Norton-Taylor, 'Blair sees security role for Russia', *The Guardian*, 17 Nov. 2001, p.9.
8. Alexander Nicoll, 'Blair seeks closer NATO ties with the Kremlin', *Financial Times*, 17 Nov. 2001, p.7.
9. Confidential interview in London in summer 2001.

Polish-Ukrainian Relations: A Strategic Relationship Conditioned by Externalities

ROMAN WOLCZUK

Historically, relations between Poland and Ukraine have, perhaps, been more 'intimate' than those between many neighbours, in so far as the former has over various periods of time incorporated significant swathes of the latter. However, following Ukraine's independence in 1991, the two neighbours sought to put this troubled past behind them and focus on forging a 'strategic' relationship. For Ukraine, stronger ties with Poland were to help avoid political isolation in the shadow of Russia with which Kiev has close but circumscribed relations. In addition, tighter relations with Poland could contribute to Ukraine's re-designation as a fully-fledged European state.

In contrast with Ukraine's unwavering stance towards Poland, the attitude of the latter towards Ukraine has ebbed and flowed according to its own international predicament, or in more technical terms, compelling externalities. Externalities are defined as benefits (positive externalities) and costs (negative externalities) that are conferred on actors other than those that are the sources of such externalities.[1] This report will highlight three externalities that conditioned Poland's stance towards Ukraine.

The first externality (a negative one for Polish-Ukrainian relations) was the threat presented by a wounded Russia. Between 1991 and 1994 when Poland's membership of key Western institutions seemed a distant prospect, Poland prioritised relations with Russia over those with Ukraine.

The second externality (a positive one for relations) emerged between 1994 and 1997 with the prospect of NATO membership for Poland. This prospect for membership required Poland to show 'regional leadership' and to strengthen its ties with Ukraine. As a result, Poland actively started to underpin Ukrainian independence – a strong, stable and genuinely independent Ukraine was the means by which Warsaw sought to ensure that it would not be the bulwark of the West.

The third externality, a negative one for relations, emerged after 1997 when prospects for Poland's membership of the EU brightened following the invitation to apply for NATO membership in July 1997. The externality lay in the fact that EU membership would impose significant impediments to the further evolution of Polish-Ukrainian relations. Each of these periods, along with their corresponding externalities will now be explored in more detail.

1991–1994: The Russian Factor

Following Ukrainian independence in 1991, both Poland and Ukraine showed themselves committed to avoiding the divisive mistakes of the past that had so despoiled relations between them. Poland was raised to a prominence in Kiev, which far exceeded that of any other Central and East European State (CEES), something which was highlighted by the Ukrainian President, Leonid Kravchuk, who stated that 'the degree of co-operation with Poland will be higher than any country of the CIS, including Russia'.[2]

Equally surprising was the statement made by the ostensibly pro-Russian Prime Minister, Leonid Kuchma, in 1993 that 'from the point of view of economic interests, Poland is our number one state'.

The feelings were, on one level, reciprocated. Pilsudski's famous statement that 'without an independent Ukraine, there cannot be an independent Poland' was quoted by the Polish President, Lech Walesa and his policy-makers on a regular basis. This positiveness was reflected in formal achievements such as the signing in May 1992, of the Treaty on Good Neighbourly and Friendly Relations and Cooperation[3] and in January 1993 the Treaty on the Legal Regime on the Ukrainian-Polish National Boundaries, Cooperation and Mutual Support on Border Issues.[4]

In practice, however, Poland remained focused on and over concerned with Russia, almost to the exclusion of Ukraine. This was particularly true as verbal hostilities between Ukraine and Russia reached a crescendo over 1992 and into 1993. Further complicating the situation for Poland was the fact that Ukraine reneged on its commitment to dismantle its nuclear arsenal (proclaimed on independence), something that made it a pariah state in the West. The problem was finally resolved at the beginning of 1994 when Ukraine committed itself to denuclearisation after having signed the Trilateral Agreement with Russia and the USA.

During this period, the underlying problem in Polish-Ukrainian relations was the fact that Poland lacked a coherent Eastern policy. Policy effectively boiled down to supporting an independent Ukraine, though not at the expense of ties with Russia. Above all, Poland was over concerned with the instability emanating from the East leading it to pursue a foreign and security policy that moved solely in response to its prospects for NATO membership, the prospects of which improved dramatically from 1994 with attendant benefits for the relationship.

1994–1997: The NATO Factor

The signing of the Trilateral Agreement between Ukraine, Russia and USA, and the end of Ukraine's pariah status removed some of the constraints on Poland, allowing it to be more overtly supportive of its Eastern neighbour. The Agreement also ended the shouting match between Ukraine and Russia, and was the start of the relative normalization of ties between them, again allowing Poland to have closer ties with the former without fear of reprisals from the latter. However, a more important factor leading to an amelioration of ties was the fact that, from 1994, Poland's prospects for NATO membership improved dramatically. And because Polish membership was at least in part dependent on an absence of Ukrainian objections, a rapprochement between the two was necessary.

This more benign and less threatening international context meant that powerful voices within Poland started to emerge calling for a new policy towards former Polish territories. The result was the development of a new Ukraine-focused *Ostpolitik* that seemed to put Ukraine at the heart of what Warsaw was trying to achieve along its eastern azimuth. Simply put, Poland wanted a stable and strong Ukraine separating Poland from Russia, but allied to if not within the Western institutional infrastructure, in so far as was possible in light of Ukraine's extensive ties with Russia.

The above factors stimulated a series of tangible improvements in military, political and economic ties between the two states. For example, in the autumn of 1995 a joint Ukrainian-Polish battalion was established, made up of the Ukrainian Mechanised Border Regiment and the Polish Przemysl 14th Tank Brigade.[5] On an economic level, the already significant growth of ties intensified with a sixfold increase in trade between 1992 and 1997.[6]

There also emerged scope for 'strategic' economic cooperation in the transportation of energy supplies. With the emergence of the Caspian region as a rich source of hydrocarbons, Poland and Ukraine were quick to see the mutual benefits of cooperating on the transportation of energy westward. There were at least three benefits that could accrue to both parties from cooperation.

First, Caspian oil offered each of them the opportunity to reduce their dependence on Russian sources.

Second, bilateral ties would be strengthened and the geopolitics of the past, whereby 'transportation networks which evolved in the last few decades isolated Poland and Ukraine from each other' would be reversed.[7]

Third, it was seen in Poland that 'the linking of transport, communication and energy networks into the pan-European networks is a prerequisite for the future integration of Ukraine into the European Union (EU) and will serve to prevent the emergence of a new line of division in Europe as Poland and Hungary enter the EU'.[8]

Progress was equally evident in the political sphere with Poland and Ukraine signing significant agreements intended to formalise the 'strategic' partnership, and at the same time send signals to various parties as to the tangible nature of this 'strategic' partnership. The signing of the Memorandum on the Liberalisation of Trade in January 1997 and the Declaration on Agreement and Unity in May 1997 were both significant in this regard.

Driving the signing of the documents was the NATO summit in July 1997 in which both neighbours sought to be involved, Poland as an invitee, Ukraine as some form of associate. The documents were thus designed to demonstrate that the two former enemies had moved towards eliminating lingering causes of disquiet and were thus ready for participation in NATO structures. The rapprochement also showed how far Poland was prepared to act in preventing the emergence of an isolated Ukraine, as a buffer between the Tashkent Treaty states and the new NATO states.

In sum, by the end of 1997, ties between Ukraine and Poland had advanced sufficiently for Leszek Balcerowicz, the Polish Economics Minister to state that 'the Polish Ministry on Foreign Affairs had reoriented itself from Russia toward Ukraine'.[9]

1997 Onwards – The EU Factor

After the successes of 1997, Warsaw was if anything even more intent on 'Europeanising' Ukraine, and bringing about Kiev's membership of Western institutions in line with Poland's policy of avoiding ending up as the bulwark of Europe. It sought to do this primarily by institutionalising the political relationship with Ukraine, as a means of sharing with Kiev its own experiences of transformation.[10]

However, while inspired to 'occidentalise' the East, Poland's foremost objective was to get into the EU. Yet this very objective required Poland to circumscribe its ties with its Eastern neighbour. In particular, Poland's preparation for membership required the adoption of the Schengen acquis in readiness for becoming the EU's external frontier and the gradual erection of a barrier between the two 'strategic' neighbours in the form of a visa regime scheduled for July 2003 without any opt outs.

This meant that Poland, as a unique area of free movement of people, was required to reverse its policy of keeping its border with Ukraine open. In sum, even prior to its own admission into Schengen, Poland was required to adopt policies that contravened its objectives vis-à-vis Ukraine. As a result, Poland's 'ambassadorial role' for Ukraine was not welcomed in the EU. Indeed, for some in the EU, it cast doubts over Poland's priorities.

Poland's predicament regarding Ukraine was compounded by two other factors.

First, Kiev repeatedly failed to implement reforms critical to its relationship with the EU, something that made Poland's life as Ukraine's 'ambassador' even more challenging.

Second, domestic developments within Ukraine once again made it the pariah of Central Europe much to the chagrin of Poland. Each will now be explored in more detail.

Ukraine's Reluctance to Introduce Reform and the Impact on Relations with the EU

Although in 1994 Ukraine signed a Partnership and Cooperation Agreement (PCA) with the EU, Ukraine pursued actions contrary to those contained within the PCA, (and the rules of the World Trade Organisation, with which the conditions of the PCA were harmonised). For example, Ukraine effectively reneged on its commitment to eliminate protectionist measures and progress toward the liberalisation of trade when it introduced unjustified certification on certain goods, tariffs and excise duties. As has been pointed out 'Ukraine's political leaders have sometimes acted as if they could achieve integration by declaration, or simply by joining and participating in international organisational and political clubs rather than by undertaking concrete structural changes'.[11]

Furthermore, question marks remain over Ukraine's commitment to the ideals of democracy, the rule of law and the promotion of human rights.

The problem for Poland lay in the fact that as Ukraine's relations with the EU failed to prosper, Poland was forced to make ever more vociferous announcements on Ukraine's behalf. Yet these efforts have not been warmly received in Western capitals. For example, Valery Giscard d'Estaing criticised the prospect of eastward enlargement so as to prevent the EU, as he put it, from sliding into a process without any spatial or temporal limits. In support of his argument he referred to a conversation he had had with the Polish president and quoted a sentence he had heard then: 'We do not want to be the Eastern border of the European Union, our neighbours to the East will have to be admitted.'[12]

In other words, not only was Ukraine's membership out of the question, but Poland's own chances of membership were being questioned. This was confirmed by Klaus Bachman who stated that 'I have heard it in German diplomatic circles that there had been Polish interventions in Berlin before the Helsinki summit, causing irritation, in the first place, to include Ukraine in the group of candidate states. One of the highest ranking members of the German government said off the record that if Poland went on like that, this was the best way to delay enlargement.'[13]

Ukraine's Internal Politics

A further factor complicating Ukraine's relations with the EU, and consequently complicating Polish-Ukrainian relations, was the deteriorating state of domestic Ukrainian politics. The corrupt nature of the 1999 presidential elections, with the incumbent and eventual winner Leonid Kuchma overtly abusing the levers of power had revealed only too clearly the extent and nature of Ukrainian politics to Brussels. However, Ukrainian politics plumbed new depths in 2000 with two events, in particular confirming Ukraine's renewed status as the pariah of Central Europe.

The first event was the ejection of the reformist Prime Minister Viktor Yushchenko. As Chairman of the National Bank of Ukraine, Yushchenko's success in presiding over the stabilisation of the economy, the introduction of the new currency, and the skilful handling of monetary policy during the Russian economic crisis in 1998, and subsequent credentials as a reformist prime minister made him a popular figure within Ukraine and highly respected by international financial institutions. However, in April 2001 oligarchic factions in Ukraine joined forces with the communists and ousted Yushchenko after passing a no confidence vote in his government. So came to an end the most successful government in the history of independent Ukraine.

Equally troubling to the West was the murder in September 2000 of Georgiy Gongadze, a Ukrainian journalist highly critical of the government. In December, conversations taped by Major Mykola Melnychenko, one of Kuchma's bodyguards, directly implicated Kuchma in the disappearance and murder of Gongadze. Almost inevitably Ukraine came to be cold-shouldered by the West in general, and the European Union in particular.[14]

Poland, alone among states to the West of Ukraine, sought to avoid the isolation of Kiev, mindful of the danger of marginalising Ukraine. However it has been said in Poland that 'at times one may actually get the impression that Poland is ready to sacrifice its own strategic interest of EU membership to drag somebody who is actually unwilling to change or reform himself forcibly to the West'.[15]

Conclusion

From Poland's point of view, Ukraine is a mission; for the EU it is merely a problem. Arguably part of the reason for Poland's failure as regards Ukraine has been Warsaw's inability to turn 'Ukraine as a Polish mission' into 'Ukraine as a European mission'. In part this may be explained by the fact that the EU lacks a geopolitical vision in the East missing as it does a coherent outlook, something that Poland claims to have.

And while Poland is relatively limited in its ability to facilitate Ukraine's 'Europeanisation', Warsaw is clearly attempting to build up its political if not economic capital in Ukraine. Poland is clearly hoping to maintain this (albeit limited) influence in Ukraine as its economic potential resurges (a relative term).

Along the Berlin–Warsaw–Kiev–Moscow axis, Poland is the smallest player. By ensuring close ties between Warsaw and Kiev, Poland is hoping that Kiev does not overlook Warsaw as the former looks Westward for capital for its renewal at some time in the future. However, in the meantime, Poland's relationship with Ukraine has been curtailed once more, in this case by the demands of Brussels. Once more, the 'strategic' relationship has been subordinated to other, 'more' strategic objectives.

NOTES

1. See D. A. Lake, 'Regional Security Complexes: A Systems Approach' in D.A. Lake and P. M. Morgan (eds.) *Regional Orders – Building Security in a New World* (Univ. Pk, PA: Pennsylvania State UP 1997) pp.45–67.
2. Ilya Prizel, 'The Influence of Ethnicity on Foreign Policy – The Case of Ukraine' in Roman Szporluk (ed.) *National Identity and Ethnicity in Russia and the New States of Eurasia* (Armonk, NY: M.E. Sharpe 1994) p.112.
3. *Ukraina na Mizhnarodniy Areni. Zbirnyk Dokumentiv I Materialiv 1991–1995. Knyha 1*, Ministerstvo Zakordonnych Sprav Ukrainy (Kiev: Yurinkom Inter 1998) p.250.

4. Ibid. p.385.
5. Y. Berdesha, M. Honchar, and O. Moskalets, *Mistse Polshchi v Polititsi Bezpeky Ukrainy* (forthcoming).
6. Z. Najder, 'Porozumienie w Schengen i Wschodni Sasiedzi Polski', in *Polska Droga do Schengen – Opinie Ekspertów* (Warsaw: Institut Spraw Publicznych 2000) p.75.
7. *Uriadovy Kurier*, 24 May 1997.
8. See Berdesha *et al.* (note 5).
9. *Zerkalo Nedeli*, 27 Dec. 1997.
10. In addition to institutions set up earlier such as the Consultative Committee of Presidents, and the Polish-Ukrainian Inter-Governmental Coordinating Council for Inter-Regional Co-operation both set up in 1993, a Polish-Ukrainian Local Government Forum and Ukrainian-Polish Parliamentary Group were established in 1999. In May 1999, a Standing Polish-Ukrainian Conference on European Integration was established with the aim of supporting the aspirations of Ukraine for participation in European integration and to share with Ukraine its experience in its transformation.
11. J. Sherr, *Ukraine's New Time of Troubles*, G67 (Camberley, UK: Conflict Studies Research Centre 1998) p.12.
12. 'Polish Policy vis-à-vis Ukraine and How it is Perceived in EU Member State' (Transcript of a Debate), Centre for International Relations, *Reports & Analyses* 2 (2000) p.3.
13. Ibid. p.5.
14. It is rumoured that at the Sept. 2001 EU-Ukraine Yalta summit, at a dinner with the Ukrainian president, EU representatives almost universally offered their apologies and excused themselves.
15. See report (note 12) p.4.

Abstracts

Continental Drift? Transatlantic Relations in the Twenty-First Century by Adrian Hyde-Price

For over half a century, the close transatlantic relationship between Europe and the USA has provided an important factor of stability and predictability in global politics and international security. Since the end of the Cold War, however, transatlantic relations have experienced some serious stresses and strains. The article examines the overall health of the contemporary transatlantic relationship in the light of the differences that have emerged over recent years. It does so by outlining four scenarios for the future of transatlantic relations in the early twenty-first century. The analysis involves three steps.

First: an assessment of the nature and foundations of the transatlantic relationship.

Second: identifying the key factors driving its current and future development.

And third: outlining scenarios for the future.

The aim of this analysis is to draw out the implications of current policies options for the transatlantic relationship and to suggest ways of managing the increasingly complex agenda facing US and European decision-makers. It then examines how these developments apply to Poland within European security.

In Search of a New Role: Poland in Euro-Atlantic Relations by Olaf Osica

The essay addresses the politics of Poland's new position as an active participant in transatlantic security. The article is divided into two major parts, with the first part looking at the cultural and historical tenets of security thinking in Poland and the second half discussing Warsaw's position towards key issues in transatlantic security. The discussion about the cultural and historical elements behind Poland's security policy identifies its predominantly defensive character, which continues to weigh heavily on Warsaw's position towards transatlantic relations. In particular, Osica investigates Poland's policies towards the future of NATO, NATO's eastern enlargement, missile defence and military intervention.

The author argues that in all of these areas Warsaw demonstrates strong Atlanticist tendencies. However, the predominantly defensive character of Poland's security policy continues to obstruct Warsaw's ambitions to become a significant player in transatlantic and European security.

Modernizing the Polish Military by Andrew A. Michta

The writer reviews the record of reform leading up to Poland's membership in NATO, as well as the country's contribution as a new ally since 1999. It discusses force reductions and a new pattern of civil-military relations in Poland in preparation for membership in NATO. Next it focuses on the most urgent current task of equipment modernization, taking as the baseline the 2001–2006 program. It argues that while Poland has largely succeeded in transforming its institutions and its civil-military relations, equipment modernization has lagged. The article concludes with a brief assessment of Poland's performance in NATO.

From Security Consumer to Security Provider – Poland and Transatlantic Security in the Twenty-First Century by Kerry Longhurst

Developments in Polish security policy have been guided since the end of the Cold War by the prospect, first, of membership in NATO and more latterly the European Union. This article appraises the current demands and expectations placed upon Poland by these two institutions and attempts to identify the nature of the role the EU and NATO wish Poland to play in the coming years. The article argues that Poland must take the necessary steps to become a 'net-provider of security', rather than a net-consumer if it is to be considered a valuable and effective partner in transatlantic security.

Poland: America's New Model Ally by David H. Dunn

This essay analyses how successful Poland has been at establishing itself as a valuable ally of the United States and on what basis that relationship is based. How solid this relationship will remain in the face of possible policy differences is also analysed. In order to do this the essay first analyses the background basis of the relationship. Against this backdrop the major policy debates which are likely to dominate the transatlantic agenda are then analysed as a way of discerning their impact on Polish-American security relations. The essay then analyses what 'added value' Poland brings to NATO from the perspectives of the American policy community. It then goes on to look at the issues of Poland's Ostpolitik; NATO Article 5; NATO Enlargement; Ballistic Missile Defence; European Security and Defence Policy, and Polish Defence Policy within NATO. How these issues contribute to making Poland America's new model ally will then be assessed.

Security and Defence in the New Europe: Franco-Polish Relations – Victim of Neglect? by Vanda Knowles

The Saint-Malo Declaration in December 1998 and NATO enlargement in March 1999 brought both France and Poland to centre stage. With both keen to forge a role for themselves within their respective contexts, the extent of their discord on security and defence issues has become more visible. France has long championed the cause of a European defence. Poland, an important player in an enlarged Europe, is a staunch ally of America and sits at the Atlanticist end of the security and defence spectrum. This article addresses the areas that appear to present the greatest sources of antagonism and, in particular, the role of rhetoric and political discourse in defining the parameters of the debate.

The German-Polish Security Partnership within the Transatlantic Context – Convergence or Divergence? by Kai-Olaf Lang

German-Polish relations are a basic element of Europe's new security architecture. German endorsement for Poland's NATO-membership is one of the most viable indicators showing the closeness of both countries' security priorities in the 1990s. Nevertheless, there have always been different perspectives and varying objectives in security matters between Berlin and Warsaw, with many of them being rooted in differing interpretations of transatlantic relations. Poland was reluctant in accepting Europe's Security and Defence Policy, has been a standard bearer of close ties with the US, has preferred a rather 'traditional' model of NATO, has been doubtful about a fast rapprochement with Russia and has emphasised the importance of Ukraine. However, it is rather improbable that those tendencies could jeopardise the emerging German-Polish security partnership. In spite of occasional friction, in the long run decreasing incongruence seems to be the more likely outcome of German-Polish security relations.

Poland and Transatlantic Relations in the Twenty-First Century by Marcin Zaborowski

This analysis presents both a summary of the volume's key arguments and a discussion of the evolution of transatlantic relations on the eve of 11 September 2001 and Poland's position in this new security context. Zaborowski argues that following the terrorist attacks on America, the transatlantic relationship has been rapidly changing. Most importantly, while NATO has been weakened by its absence in Afghanistan, security has been increasingly 'nationalised' – a tendency apparent in the US's and individual European states' responses to the crisis. These developments add some urgency for Poland to take upon itself the role of being a security provider and to reform its defence sector thoroughly by switching from territorial defence to fully professional and more mobile forces.

About the Contributors

Adrian Hyde-Price, Dept. of Politics, University of Leicester, UK.

Olaf Osica, European University Institute, Florence, Italy.

Andrew A. Michta, International Studies Dept., Rhodes College, Memphis, Tennessee, USA.

Kerry Longhurst, Institute for German Studies, European Research Institute, University of Birmingham, UK.

David H. Dunn, Dept. of Political Science and International Studies, University of Birmingham, UK.

Vanda Knowles, Institute for German Studies, University of Birmingham, UK.

Kai-Olaf Lang, Stiftung Wissenschaft und Politik, Berlin.

Marcin Zaborowski, Dept. of Languages and European Studies, Aston University, Birmingham, UK.

Silke Pottebohm, Institute for German Studies, European Research Institute, University of Birmingham, UK.

Roman Wolczuk, University of Wolverhampton, UK.

Index